WHEN –
カメラがクレージー

Culture Club
カルチャー・クラブ

CAMERAS GO

Kasper de Graaf : Malcolm Garrett
カスパー・ド・グラフ　マルコム・ガレット

AVENUE
IERLAND NU
EEN VISUEEL PORTRET
HYPNOSE
VAN MAGISCH RITUEEL TOT MEDISCH INSTRUMENT
RITUELEN
INDRINGEND FRAGMENT UIT EEN NIEUWE ROMAN VAN CEES NOOTEBOOM
BLITZ
NA PUNK EN DISCO

音楽一週
music week

NEW MUSICAL EXPRESS
NME
WOULD YOU SLEEP WITH A BOY LIKE THIS?
JOHN LE CARRÉ MILES DAVIS GIL SCOTT-HERON

THE FACE
THAT BOY GEORGE!
WHAM!
NU
SHAKIN'STEVENS
Culture Club
TÆT PÅ SNEAKERS
JOHN LENNON -DEN REBELSKE BEATLE
E.T.
ÅRETS MUSIKNAVN?
POPCORN
POSTER
SZENE DEUTSCHLAND
NEUE STARKE FILME!
BOY GEORGE
SOFT CELL
TOYAH
SHAKATAK
salut!
CULTURE CLUB
TOUTE LA VERITE SUR
BOY GEORGE
UN MINI JOURNAL CLAUDE FRANÇOIS
KAREN CHERYL
SUPER TONIC
LES FORBANS
A LONDRES AVEC
BANANARAMA
TELEPHONE LE PORTRAIT ROBOT DE JEAN-LOUIS
HIGELIN INEDIT
KLAXON
BUZY
ALEXANDRE
STERLING
להיטון
הליצנים
pop Rocky
CHARTBUSTERS
CULTURE CLUB
TEARS FOR FEARS
DURAN DURAN
BLANCMANGE
MODERN ROMANCE
BANANARAMA
COMPETITIONS
FREE INSIDE 2 BIG CALENDARS
Smash HITS
CULTURE CLUB
FREE INSIDE
NICK HEYWARD
THE JAM
WIN A WALKMAN
KID CREOLE · ADAM ANT

BRAVO
Land in Sicht?
Udo auf Odyssee-Tourn
ich hab' schon mal gelebt
„RAMBO"
Autogrammkarte
BOY GEORGE POSTER
Musik Szene
Nr. 1 / Januar 1983
DM 2,80
SUPERTRAMP
WHITESNAKE
TANGERINE DREAM
TOM PETTY & HEARTBREAKERS
WISHBONE ASH
MEN AT WORK
JOHNNY WARMAN
GEORGE THOROGOOD
PHIL LYNOTT
LONDON'S KULTURSCHOCK: CULTURE CLUB
EXTRABREIT — Tournee- und Filmpläne
ABC — 6 Shows im Jan./Febr.
OKEJ
Nr 4
1983
14 dagar
KIM WILDE
SAXON
NINA HAGEN
TOTO COELO
HANOI ROCKS
MICK JAGGER
ACE FREHLEY
MARI WILSON
PAT BENATAR
HALL & OATES
SIMPLE MINDS
NOICE & HASSE
RICHARD GERE
NIELS JENSEN
NIKLAS WAHLGREN
LEIGH McCLOSKEY
SYLVESTER STALLONE
BOY GEORGE
CULTURE CLUB
MADNESS
WENDY
PLASMATICS
KAJAGOOGOO • ULTRAVOX • U2 • GRACE JONES
RECORD MIRROR
CULTURE CLUB
Exclusive!
HEY! ELASTICA
TALK TALK
MAN PARRISH
SHRIEKBACK
LAUREL AND HARDY
Pop on TV — a ruthless exposé
JOEPIE
10 JAAR
Ekstra Gratis fanclub lidkaart
2 stunt wedstrijden
Win reis met Eurosong winnaar
Boy George ontmaskerd
BRAVO
Große Verlosung:
Souvenirs
E.T.
Spiel mit dem Übersinnlichen:
Pendle Dein Glück!
Gold-Otto:
NENA &
SHAKY
CULTURE CLUB
Aufklärung:
Orgasmus
WEEK 2
HITKRANT
HUMAN LEAGUE
PHIL COLLINS
Kim Wilde's geheime romance
GENE SIMMONS
Bananarama
Bucks Fizz
Het grote Boy George geheim
J. GEILS BAND • PRINCE • TIME
VANITY 6 • HAYSI FANTAYSEE
vi unge
nyt
Særpris: 11,50 kr.
GIGANT DOBBELT PLAKAT (57x92)
MOD
BOY GEORGE
ELO
KIM WILDE
PHIL OAKEY
STOR GLAD KONKURRENCE MED DEJLIGE GEVINSTER
LOKKEDE MIG TIL AT SMIDE TØJET
E.T.
Boy George
FANs Se Her
BUCKS FIZZ • SHAKIN' STEVENS • VOXPOP • GO-GO's • ZAPPA
DONNA
eccentricity and transvestitism
from all over the world
nights full of madness and cheer

カルチャー・クラブ

NOISE!
FREE FLEXI culture club & blue rondo
★ THE JAM
★ BELLE STARS
★ THE BANSHEES
★ FAD GADGET
★ THE CLASH
★ THE THE
★ CHARGE
& features

OCTOBER 16, 1982 35p WEEKLY/USA $2
MM
CULTURE CLUB
Features
THE DAMNED · GUN CLUB · CROWN HEIGHTS AFFAIR · MARK STEWART · KATE BUSH · PULSALLAMA · THE JUNGLE ·
Albums
JOAN JETT · ULTRAVOX · FOUR TOPS ·
Live
PSYCHEDELIC FURS · TEARDROPS · DEXYS · JOHN MARTYN · SAXON · GBH · AU PAIRS · ANTI-PASTI · WILLIAM BURROUGHS ·
PLAYBACK: THE FLEXI
FOUR-TRACK SINGLE PLUS FREE ALBUM OFFER
ALLAN JONES GOES HEADBANGING IN SEARCH OF HEAVY METAL

Now In Our 13th Year & STILL FREE!
SCENE
ENTERTAINMENT WEEKLY
CULTURE CLUB
A CONVERSATION WITH BOY GEORGE
BERLIN

ビバ・ロック
VIVA ROCK
Enjoy!! Gossipy Entertainment Magazine 1983 NO.10
1983 4

MIT JAHRES-HOROSKOP '83
BRAVO
Gasgeben ist das Geilste!
CULTURE CLUB
Gold für SPIDER MURPHY GANG
E.T. Woher er stammt

50p July 29-August 4
Event
The London entertainment guide
Rock
Jazz
Clubs & Discos
Film
Theatre
TV & Radio
Betting
Eating Out
The Arts
Classical
Dance
Shopping
Pubs & Bars
Travel
Video
Sue Clowes & Culture Club
Dr Who & Simon Napier Bell

1

ザ・ショー・ビギンズ

the show begins

˜t is March 31st, 1983. Outside London's Dominion Theatre the traffic bustles past, up Tottenham Court Road and home, preparing perhaps set off again for the Easter Bank Holiday that's just begun. Centre Point, wering remnant of a carefree past, fails to cast a shadow over the new nfidence that surges below.

At around 7pm, the pubs begin to fill with crowds of young people in atmosphere of extravagance and excitement as they have a drink fore the show. Two ambulances pull up outside the theatre and park ere to serve both as warning and reassurance to the high-spirited fans. night The Dominion is sold out; the swarming ticket touts are the only pe left for those who didn't book well in advance.

The band that's generated all this interest is one whose impact on hit cord charts has been unequalled in the last five months. This band has ocked and outraged decent citizens everywhere, yet its music is loved grannies and little children alike. Its lead singer, who once set out to be e most outrageous person in London, became every mother's wayward n – and his message to his fans is: you're not the only freak out there. true to yourself and don't be fooled by what you see. Things are rarely hat they seem . . .

2

ルーマーズ オブ・ロマンス

rumours of romance

˜t was the third single that did it for Culture Club. The first two, White Boy and I'm Afraid Of Me, had done little more than establish that the nd were competent musicians and that the lead singer, Boy George, ew what to do with a voice.

This in itself was no mean achievement. London had been suffering from an overdose of rumour bands – stylish outfits drawn from nightclub regulars who tended to play only to exclusive gatherings of their peers until a massive deal was signed with some desperate record company. At the start of the decade, the music business was tired and its scouts (known as A&R men because they work in the Artists & Repertoire departments) seemed incapable of finding strong new acts to stimulate the record-buying public. Everyone was looking for the Next Big Thing.

The rumour approach worked for its pioneers, Spandau Ballet, whose manager Steve Dagger devised his 'by-the-clubs, of-the-clubs, for-the-clubs' strategy to distinguish his band from the music business machine and to demonstrate a groundswell of support on the streets. But it backfired on those who tried to follow in Dagger's footsteps. The exclusiveness that had been designed to separate the bands from the industry, instead came to be viewed as elitism that separated them from their audience. The most notable casualty was Blue Rondo A La Turk, whose undoubted musical talents failed to produce the instant success that was widely anticipated. Instead, the Latin bandwagon with which they had become identified was hijacked by singalong popsters Modern Romance, who had no such problem as having to live up to street credibility.

Associations with fashion and clubs – or the 'new romantic' scene, as it was soon dubbed – thus became a potential handicap, particularly as the out-of-touch rock weeklies pounced on every available opportunity to scream "Style Over Content!"

On the face of it, any band fronted by Boy George was the very epitome of a rumour band. In association with designer Sue Clowes, Culture Club projected what was easily the strongest clothing range of 1981, using colourful fabric designs with tramp symbols and religious imagery to produce such items as the outrageous 'Sex In Heaven' T-shirt. George had been a favourite with magazine photographers and gossip columnists for some time. He'd even had a brief association with the King of Rock'n'Roll Swindlers, Malcolm McLaren, when he sang together with Annabella Lu Win in BowWowWow. He ranked with the nation's chief nightclub posers alongside Steve Strange, Martin Degville, Pete Burns and Philip Salon. More even than Steve Strange, George was the face of new romanticism.

Everyone knew that George could shock. Everyone knew he had a fine dress sense and a pretty radical eye for make-up. Almost everyone who'd met him knew he had a quick temper and a sharp tongue. But very few people knew he could sing. And no-one knew he could write lyrics to melt even the coldest heart.

White Boy and I'm Afraid of Me lifted the veil. Even though their impact on the charts was slight, they created the first, hardcore following for Culture Club. They showed, moreover, that this band combines the experience and creative talents of four very different individuals.

The break came in November 1982, when the third single, Do You Really Want To Hurt Me?, raced to the top spot in the British singles chart and stayed there for three weeks. The BBC's national easy-listening station, Radio 2, named it Record of the Week. George caused uproar in an outraged national press. "Wally of the Week!" screamed one paper. "The Gender Bender!" declared another.

WATCH IT! by NINA MYSKOW

The TV column that puts you in the picture

WALLY OF THE WEEK

IT WAS a wally, all right. But just *what was it?* Ther[e] must have been millions of homes split by strife an[d] divided by debate when John Peel introduced Culture Club on Top Of The Pops.

Up on the screen loomed The Thing, singing Do You Really Want To Hurt Me?

Well, not really, but you did ask for it . . . beautifully made up and wearing a tunic dress with trousers, it proceeded to prance about gracefully.

There were shades of the horrible creep from Haysi Fantayzee—thankfully without the understains—but it was impossible to tell from voice or prance whether The Thing was male or female.

The record company say it was male—Boy George to be precise.

Frankly I don't give a damn. I've got Culture shock.

Boy George

3

バース・オブ・ア・ボーイ

birth of a Boy

rouble was no stranger to the O'Dowd household in South
. London, but perhaps it was allocated more than its fair
are on June 14th, 1961.

On that date, Diana O'Dowd was delivered of a bouncing
by Boy at Bexley Hospital, and she named him George Alan.
was the third son in this Irish Catholic family that was later
mpleted with two further sons and a daughter.

At that hopeful hour in 1961 no-one anticipated that, one
y, toasters would be flying through the kitchen; that this boy
ould love one minute and hate the next; that (encouraged by
nt Josie) he'd walk around in lurex cat suits and ridiculously
gh platform shoes; that he would cause untold embarrass-
ent and be expelled from school. The first 15 years of George
Dowd's life were enough to stretch the patience of even the
ntliest parents beyond breaking point.

Times were hard as George grew up. His father Jeremiah,
ormer soldier, struggled to earn enough from the building
de to support his rapidly growing brood. Church every
nday was welcome relief from the conditions back home at
n Crescent, Eltham, where mum and dad occupied one
droom, little sister Siobhain another, and all the boys
chard, Kevin, George, Gerald and David) the third. The two
atians did little to maintain sanity in the home.

While George was still too young to inflict serious
mage, domestic problems tended to centre on eldest brother
hard, whose skinhead period brought him into frequent
nflict with the police — and with his parents.

By the early 70s, when Richard was into the Clockwork
ange 'droog' look, George's own obsession with music and
thes was well under way. He fell in love with Marc Bolan —
uring Indian shops for embroidered jackets, cheesecloth
rts and flared trousers with velvet cut-outs; much to the
nsternation of Mrs Crome (his friend's mum) he went to
nday school dressed in a camel-hair coat, a big floppy hat,
tform shoes, flared trousers and a cravat; he went to concerts
David Cassidy, David Essex and — "the biggest thing, it was
illiant" — David Bowie in 1973.

At first his parents tried to curb his excesses (during the
lan period he wasn't allowed to corkscrew his hair), but
entually they adopted other tactics. "One day my mum came
ck from Petticoat Lane," remembers George, "and she'd
ught me these HUUUGE platforms — for school! I thought

she'd really gone off her rocker. She said, right, go to school in *them*. I did. And I got sent home."

By this time, mum had finally got fed up with the authorities' failure to respond to her pleas for a bigger house, so instead of paying the rent to the council, she paid it into a savings account. The tactic worked: when threats of legal action had no effect, the council finally provided the O'Dowds with a larger house a few miles north of Joan Crescent, at Shooters Hill. "It was like a dream," George recalls. "We still had three bedrooms, but it was massive."

Pressure on space was further relieved by the fact that Richard fell out with mum and disappeared for seven years.

Left to right: Kevin, Gerald, Richard, Boy and first girlfriend Denise Higgins

What an exciting moment,
Yet your hearts were filled with joy,
When the doctor beamed upon you
And announced "You have a Boy!"

4

ボーイ・トーク(1)

Boy talk (1)

"When we were young, my father was quite strict. He had a lot of problems: he didn't have any money, he left the army and he had all these bloody kids. He was a builder and he had a really hard time for years, until his business started doing well.

"At school, the kids used to go to the chip shop for dinner, but if *we* did that, we'd get killed. We weren't allowed to eat anything that wasn't good for us. My parents always used to make us eat great big meals.

"Having six kids, my father and mother didn't show any emotion at all towards me. And all the time, that's what I wanted. I wanted to kiss my father, I wanted affection. My father used to come back and take his aggression out on us because he'd had a hard day at work. I hated him then.

"I was the sort of kid that, if I thought he was wrong, I'd say, I hate you, you're wrong. My father used to say, you've got no right to answer me back; and I'd say, I have, you're wrong. I was really dogmatic when I was a kid. I was awful.

"And my mother, I used to hound her. I had this period when I was about 14 where if I had to go to school I'd eat my breakfast really slowly and I'd say, I'm having breakfast, I'm not going to school on an empty stomach, I'll be ill. I'd be slowly eating and my mother would say — get out that door! And I'd go, no, hang on a minute. There used to be flakes flying across the kitchen. One morning she threw the toaster at me, she shouted GET OUT, GET OUT! And I'd go, I hate you, so she'd say, wait till your father gets in, your father is going to see you.

"And I was going, I'm not fucking coming back, you bitch, I hate you. Then I'd go up the road and think, oh my god, I'm gonna get killed, I just swore at her.

"I used to fight with my dad. He used to hit my little brothers when we were sitting at the dinner table, and I'd just throw my dinner on the floor and say, I hate you. So he'd say, what did you do that for? And I'd say, because you hit him and you've no right, you did it for no reason. Then someone else would say, yeah, you shouldn't have hit him and my dad would say, you're fucking causing trouble in this house!...

"Sometimes he'd say, here son, get me that. And I'd

Clockwise from top: Uncle Alan, brother Kevin and wife Sheena, sister Siobhain, Mum, Aunt Tina and Aunt Teresa. Centre of attention: George

, get it yourself — and he just used to go mad and run up road after me. Then I'd say, all the trouble it's taken ı to chase after me, you could have done it yourself.

"He was violent, my dad — but basically he's a very ely person, you know what I mean? I do really love ı, but he just didn't know when to stop.

"Eventually, when I was about 14, I thought right, I ı't want you to love me, I don't want any affection from ı at all. One day I had this massive fight with my dad I locked myself in the bathroom. Well, he smashed the r down and I tripped and cut myself. He didn't really an to hurt me, because by the time he'd kicked the door vn, he'd calmed down.

"It wasn't that bad, but it looked bad at the time, and dad went, oh my god, what have I done? And I went, ht, that's it, I hate you. And I ran out of the house and yed at my friend Ruth's. Her mum's quite a liberal old v, she used to let me do what I liked. So I stayed there two weeks.

"I was quite lonely, because I really loved my ther, you know what I mean? I used to really get on h her on my good days. And I did like my dad too, ause I liked his attitude. I like people getting angry. I e no emotion.

Boy and Parents

ıool Boy

"Anyway, one day my mum phoned up and said, come back. I said, I don't want to come back ever again. (I did really, but I just thought, I'm not gonna make a fuss.) My dad came on the phone and he said, come back, it'll be all right.

"And when I went back it was fine. It was really weird, but my dad changed completely from that day on. And now he's brilliant. It's weird, but I can kiss him now. I couldn't when I was a kid — and that sort of thing, you really want to do it when you can't, you know what I mean?"

5

ザ・グリーンハウス

the greenhouse

When the family first moved to Shooters Hill, George was what you might call a real Seventies Groover. Then, just before his 14th birthday, he met Tracie Birch.

Tracie, her own style projected by an outrageous, green Vidal Sassoon haircut, set about influencing George's appearance. She succeeded in transforming him in the space of that summer holiday in 1975. The teachers who had no doubt been relieved at taking a break from this long-haired, platform-heeled, flared-trousered apparition in June, must have thought they'd come back to the wrong place when in September they were faced with a New Age Kid with a bright orange trowel haircut, white plastic sandals, drainpipe trousers, a satchel, a tie cut in half and sewn smaller by mum, and a collarless shirt. "Of course," he says now, "everybody was taking the piss."

If his parents found it difficult to manage George at times, the school authorities found it impossible. He often played truant and his demeanour was considered rude. Inevitably he ended up in the class of last resort — the Greenhouse at the top of the school, supervised by a psychologist. The children who were sent here were almost beyond redemption. They were permitted to occupy themselves, to draw, doodle or read, but they weren't allowed out of the room.

"I just used to sit there all day," says George. "You know what psychologists are like when they think they've got one up on you. They weren't supposed to let you annoy them, but I used to annoy him so much. I used to sit there saying, you're so ugly, I hate your guts. Everybody used to swear in this class, it was where you went to go *aaaaaaargh!* You were no good, you couldn't go anywhere in the school. That was it, you were a complete has-been."

In such an environment, it's not surprising that the school lost whatever attractions or relevance it might have held for George. He stayed away with increasing regularity, choosing instead to spend the days sitting in the woods.

One fateful Monday, George did go to school — though naturally he turned up late. When he walked in, he bumped into the headmaster.

"Why are you late?" he recalls the head asking.

"Because I got up late," replied George, truthful and to the point as ever.

"It's probably," the head declared, "because of all the

With Tracie Birch — "my weirdest girlfriend"

Boy and Marina

rk you did on Friday."

"I wasn't here on Friday."

"I know, goddam you, I saw you in the High Street."

"You never," said George, but his hopes of bluffing nself out of this one were fading fast.

"I bloody well did, I recognised your hair."

In the headmaster's estimation, only one punishment uld do: the cane. In the past, George had always refused to ept corporal punishment and he did so again on this asion: "No way. I don't have to take the cane off you. I don't nt to be at this school. I don't like it, I want to go home. I 't want to learn anything else."

George was given till that afternoon to change his mind, all efforts by teachers to persuade him were futile. At the of the day, he had to go home and tell his parents that he to be expelled.

There was one further ordeal to come before Boy George's ominious school career came to an end. The following week went back to school with his mum and they faced the staff ether.

"So they were talking to her and she just turned round to and said, do you want to come back here or not? Are you ng to work? And I said, no, I'm not going to work. So she ned to them and said, right, he doesn't want to be here, so leave. They said, what do you mean? She said, we leave.

"She was a bit unfriendly with me on the bus ne. . . But basically she accepted the fact that I didn't want to t. She understood me, you know what I mean?"

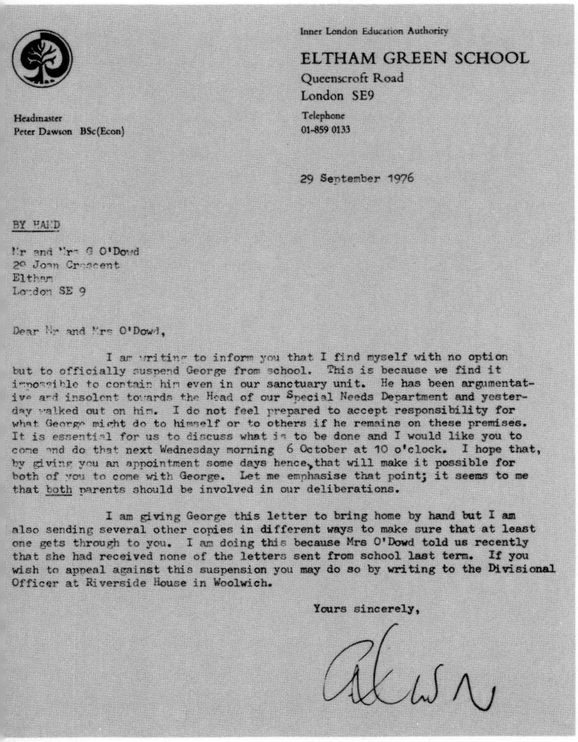
Inner London Education Authority

ELTHAM GREEN SCHOOL
Queenscroft Road
London SE9

Telephone
01-859 0133

Headmaster
Peter Dawson BSc(Econ)

29 September 1976

BY HAND

Mr and Mrs G O'Dowd
29 Joan Crescent
Eltham
London SE 9

Dear Mr and Mrs O'Dowd,

I am writing to inform you that I find myself with no option but to officially suspend George from school. This is because we find it impossible to contain him even in our sanctuary unit. He has been argumentative and insolent towards the Head of our Special Needs Department and yesterday walked out on him. I do not feel prepared to accept responsibility for what George might do to himself or to others if he remains on these premises. It is essential for us to discuss what is to be done and I would like you to come and do that next Wednesday morning 6 October at 10 o'clock. I hope that, by giving you an appointment some days hence, that will make it possible for both of you to come with George. Let me emphasise that point; it seems to me that both parents should be involved in our deliberations.

I am giving George this letter to bring home by hand but I am also sending several other copies in different ways to make sure that at least one gets through to you. I am doing this because Mrs O'Dowd told us recently that she had received none of the letters sent from school last term. If you wish to appeal against this suspension you may do so by writing to the Divisional Officer at Riverside House in Woolwich.

Yours sincerely,

ading for the end of George's school career. His dad ote on the envelope: "Stage 1. George is expelled. reer continues?"

6
ボーイ・トーク(2)

Boy talk (2)

"My first experience with a girl was with this girl called Brenda, who grabbed hold of me at my brother's party. I'd never kissed a girl and she kissed me. It was, like, wow, I've kissed a girl, I've done it, now I can do it all the time. And to me it was no big deal. I then had a girlfriend called Shelley Hughes who I was really in love with, she really grabbed my heart.

With Shelley — "my longest-lasting girlfriend"

"I started going to gay clubs when I was 14 or 15. That was the only real club scene that existed at that time and the whole pre-punk crowd went to those clubs regardless of sexual preference as they were less than welcome in their local pubs. I'd go to a club called Visuals on a gay night and people used to come up to me and say,

With Lorraine

Boy and Hilda

do you want to come home with me? And I'd laugh. think, it's disgusting, but it's funny, you know wha mean? It's a giggle. Like, I'm doing all these things an shouldn't be doing them. I used to tell my mum I w staying at my friend's.

"And then I thought, why does someone like me to a gay club? Because I don't relate to it, I don't belie people should live their sexuality.

"I met people from school occasionally. I met t bloke who used to beat me up. I was in this gay club and walked into the toilets and I thought, if this doesn't say all — you know what I mean, say it with flowers . . .

"Then there was this friend of mine, Michael. won't mention his second name — Michael X. I used know him when I was a kid and I went over to see h when I'd left school. He was into Bowie and I really lik him, because he was like ugbug and everybody w horrible to him. Anyway, he'd just got his first j uptown and his mother said to me, a man tried to mol him in the station!

"Oh my god, you know, this is like, teapot dram

"But this is the funniest bit. When I lived in Good Street with Mad Jean a few years later, I walked round t road and who should I see but this raving queen wit dog, a poodle right, and it's him! I said, oh my god, y look such a queer! And he said, I know, I am. And he liv round the corner with this black bloke.

"All these things, they're experience. It's amazi that the world is so small and we're all so naive. I think you can learn a few things, by mistakes and also by j living a bit, you know, it's great."

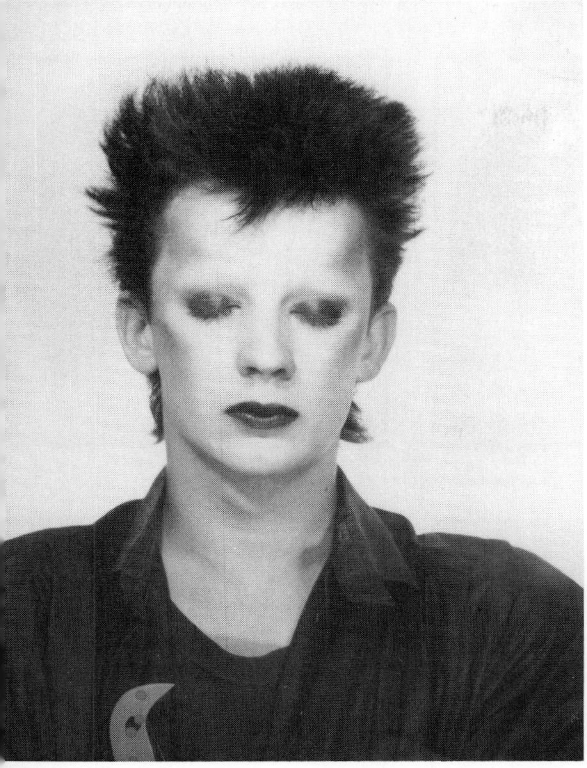

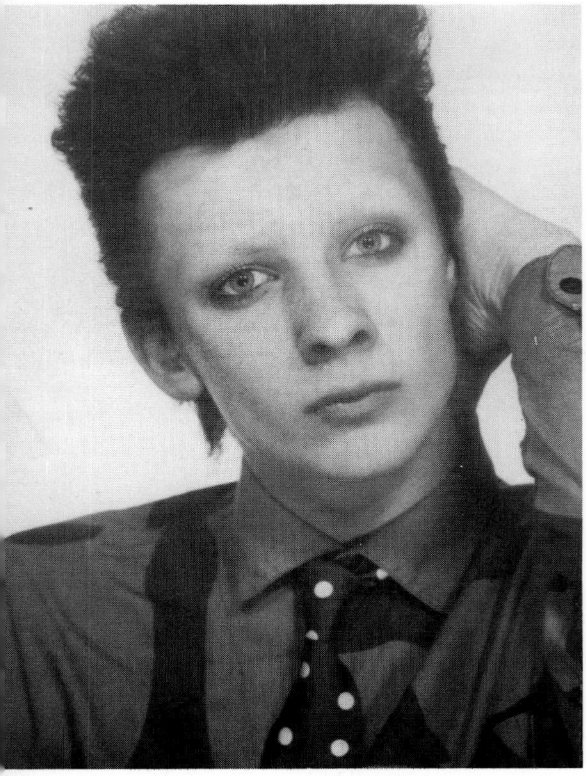

George "with a cheap Antony Price look from Oxfam. I had padded socks for my shoulders. Of course, it was well before Ronny."

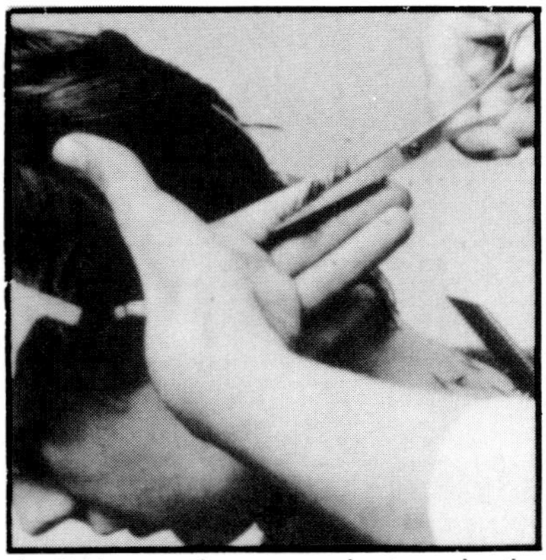

4. Taking sections upwards towards the crown, Graham here shows the previous guideline section underneath the one he is cutting

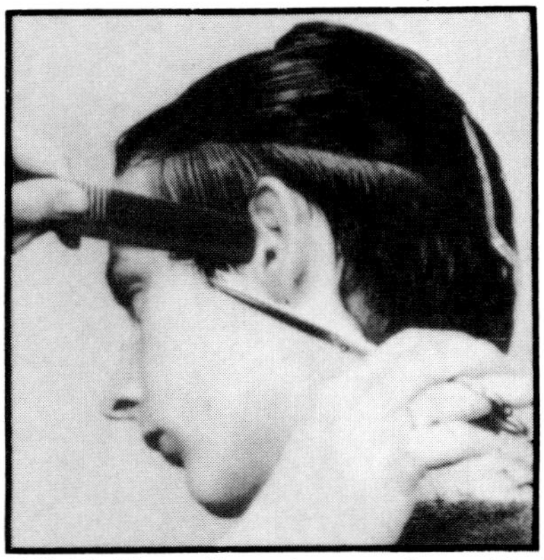

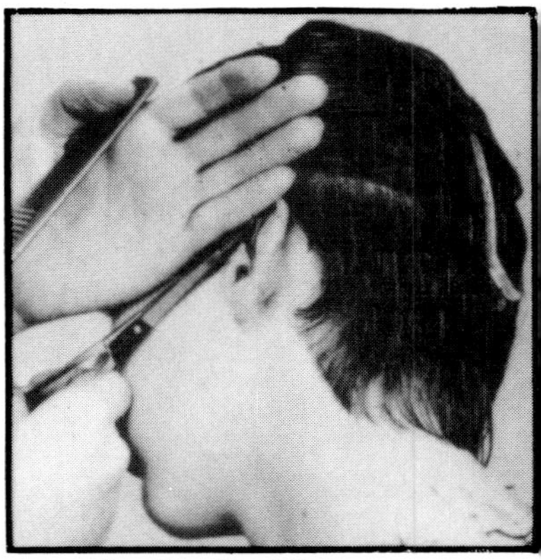

5/6. Working well past the centre for a guide, he moves to the other side of the ear. Here he moves to the front, angling the hair over the ear as shown

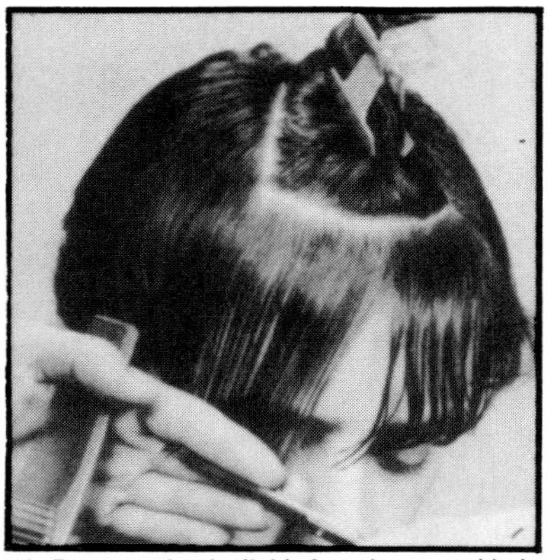

10. Front section is divided as shown and hair is combed forward to cut first left-hand section

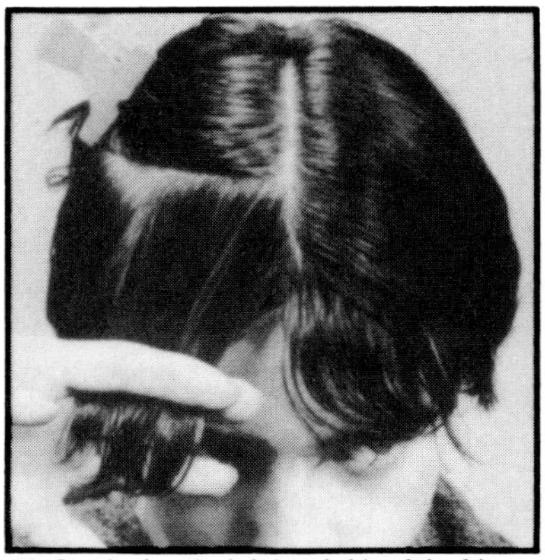

11. Continuing the left-hand side of the fringe, a new centre parting is made to ease front sectional cutting up to the crown to blend in with sides

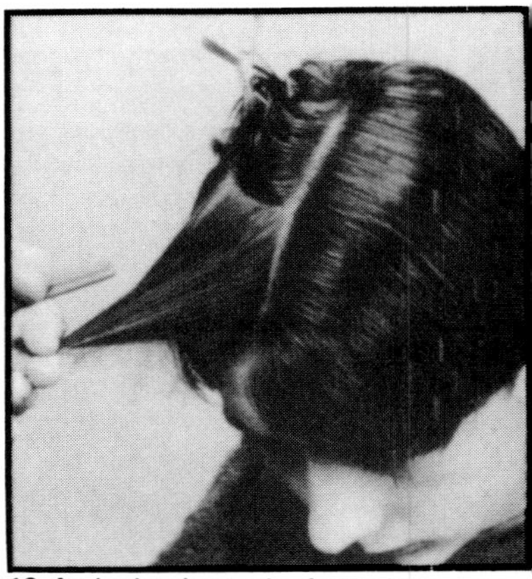

12. Again showing angle of cut taken

Blow-drying is with the fingers as cut ensures style falls into place easily

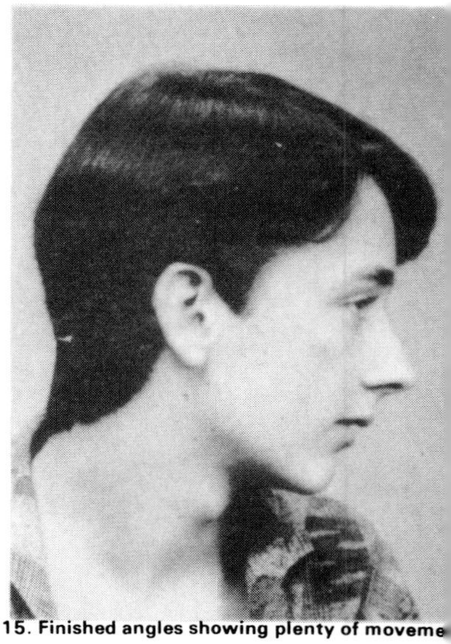

15. Finished angles showing plenty of moveme

. Finished angles showing plenty of movement

ɛehive Boy c. '79, with Patrick (Lizzy Black)

7

ザ・テスコ・プリンス

the tesco prince

Shaguarama's, Louise's, the Global Village, the Goldmine on Canvey Island and the Black Prince in Bexleyheath — these were among the clubs George visited regularly from the age of 14 — sleeping on a train at Waterloo when convenient.

"It was basically a Bowie thing," he says of the atmosphere at that time. "When Bowie was around, and Bryan Ferry, everybody used to go and see them. When Bowie came back from America we all went to see him at the station and you didn't realise how many weird people there were till you went."

At 15, his friend Jane introduced him to Troy, who ran a clothes shop called Shades in the Chelsea Antique Market on the King's Road. It was just as punk was starting. Acme Attractions and Sex (now World's End) had recently opened their doors. Some people were wearing punk, but Shades supplied winklepickers and Glen Miller suits for alternative dressers.

George started working at the shop and met Bob Marley, who was friendly with Troy. On the bus to work, he also met a little boy with curly hair who said to him, I like your hair; so George took him to a party together with a crowd of people, including "Myra Hindley from the Warren Street lot." The boy was Jeremy Fantayzee (who these days calls himself Jeremiah after George's father).

With Jeremy

Boy and Hilda

After his stint at Shades, George tried working at Tesco's, t he was sacked after a week because of the way he dressed. ey can't have realised he was a walking advertisement. He d Jane used to cover themselves in dog chains and, at the ack Prince, George would sit with Tesco bags around him and mmies in his ears.

One night he went to a club called Bangs and saw a eature with black lips, horns, a skirt, a black paper collar, pit ots and leather gloves. "He was just dancing about in this and hought, that guy looks brilliant. I immediately felt affection · him. **Nobody** looked like that then, believe me." He saw m again at Louise's wearing a jacket with Malteser wrappers over it, a top hat, suspenders and shorts — and getting anged in the middle of the dance floor. This same person was at the Sex Pistols' first gig, where he dressed as Hilda Ogden hot pants and played stuff from *The Sound of Music.*

George now describes Philip Salon as his oldest and best end. "He gave me a lot of confidence. He hates violence and doesn't lie. I think I've got quite a lot of my attitudes from m.

"It was really unusual to meet someone who didn't lie or al when you came from knowing the sort of people I knew. had such a brilliant nature. He doesn't hurt people, he esn't skip his trainfare — I thought, what a weird guy!

"He was the first person I ever saw with a binliner on. He id that he and this girl went to a nudist camp and they were o shy to show their bodies off. That's how all that started."

Punk took root. "Everybody was dressing up," George members, "and suddenly it was punk rock. Suddenly you arted getting punched in the mouth. Everywhere you went, u got hit."

n the Roxy toilets: Lorraine, Laura and George

The punks tolerated Teds in their clubs, but the reverse was not true. So, as Shooters Hill crawled with Teds, George decided to discard his newly-acquired punk look, draw on a moustache, cultivate a quiff and become a Ted — at least in dress: "I loved looking like a Ted, it was brilliant. I just hated their attitude."

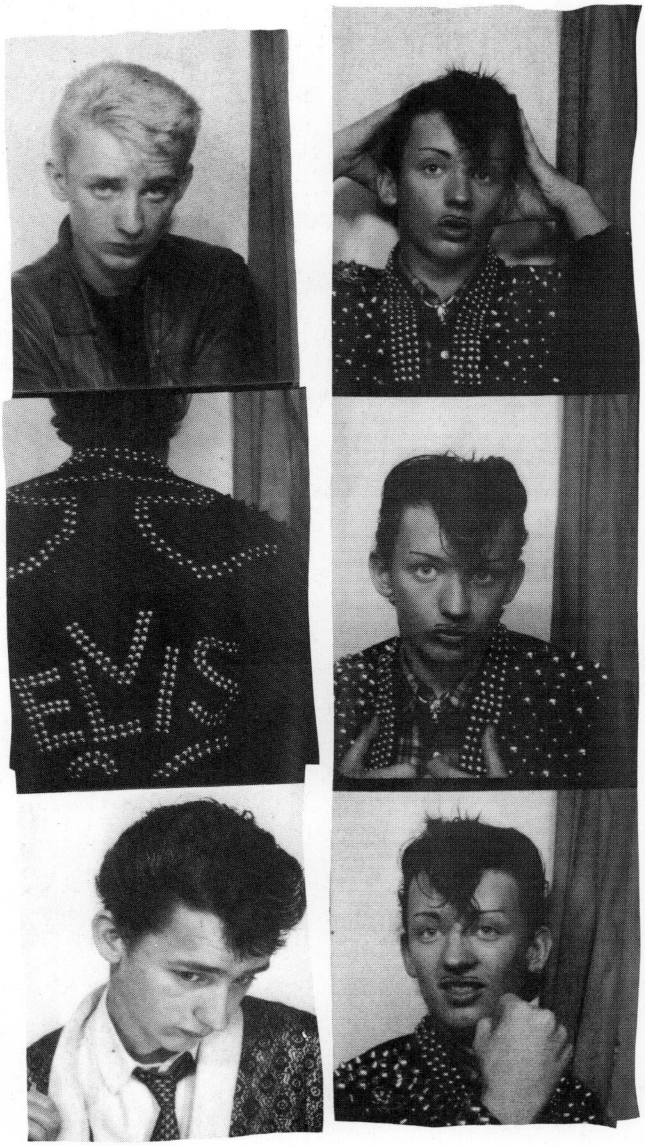

The new look was at least partly inspired by another outrageous dresser whom George had met in Southend: Martin Degville, who at this time sported an enormous white quiff and a fine moustache. The encounter was the start of another formative friendship. George was having a bad time in London, so he moved up to Birmingham and shared a flat with Martin and a couple of girls.

"I loved it up there," he says. "Birmingham was great. I had Martin to compete with, so I just went over the top. We had

At Bowie gig

With Martin Degville at the Holy City Zoo, Birmingham

With Patti Bell in Birmingham

a great time. My hair was mauve and I had it in a plait wit another bit down here. I used to go out with a green face, or blue face and a red neck. Martin and me used to be like the ugl sisters."

Martin, whose Ya Ya partnership with Jane Farrimon has since made a notable impact on developing clothing style was then taking his first steps on the road to combining clothe design with business. He opened a stall in Birmingham's Oasi market and, at George's suggestion, called it Degville' Dispensary.

After a year, George moved back to London. He starte picking up from where he'd left off and quickly made nev friends, among them Marilyn — "*the* Marilyn, you know. H was a little soul boy when I first met him, I remember I though he was a right little wally. And the next time I saw him he had dress on, a stuffed padded bra, crimped hair and eyelashes – and he was simply outrageous."

Rusty Egan and Steve Strange were just starting Billy' then — Rusty playing electronic and funky dance sounds, an Steve standing guard over who came in at the door. George needless to say, had no trouble getting in.

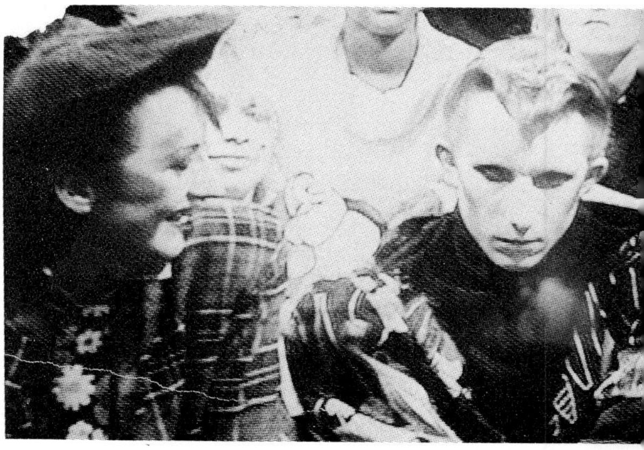

With Martin Degville on TV programme Something Else

iss Binny, George and Marilyn at the première of Breaking Glass

‘I like to dress this way all the time’

peedway Horrors
noving into
he fast lane

With Steve Strange at Billy's, 1978

·h Julia

At the Blitz with Stephen Linard, 1979

THEY LIVE  TO DRESS

th Blue Rondo's Christos at the Blitz, 1979

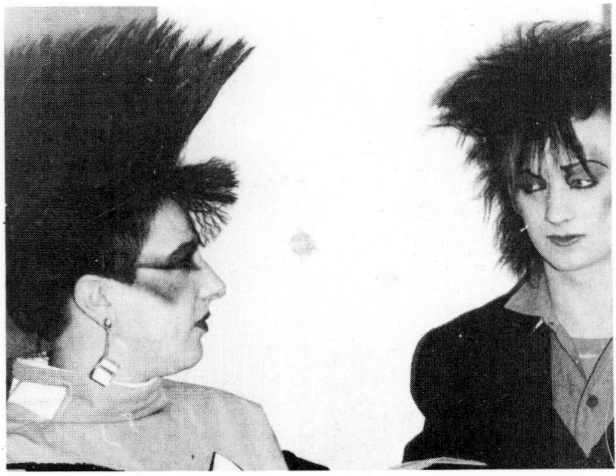

With Melissa Caplan — "I did her hair for her"

At home with punks, 1979

"The way I d

·lissa Caplan clothes*

·vents me from getting work"

" On the way to our interview, **George O'Dowd** and I called in at Harrods food hall. Everyone, customers and assistants, stopped and stared and nudged each other and winked and giggled and whispered. It was extraordinary. The energy made my hackles rise; and when a scruffy young woman came and stood a yard away and stared at George and said in a loud voice that she couldn't tell whether it was a he, she or it, my protective instincts overcame me and I told her she was being most impolite. My snooty remonstrance took her aback; then I suddenly realised that George had been thoroughly enjoying himself. He'd been loving all the hysterical attention "

In Heaven 1980, left to right: Sue, Myra, Boy, John, Marilyn, Philip Salon and Dyke

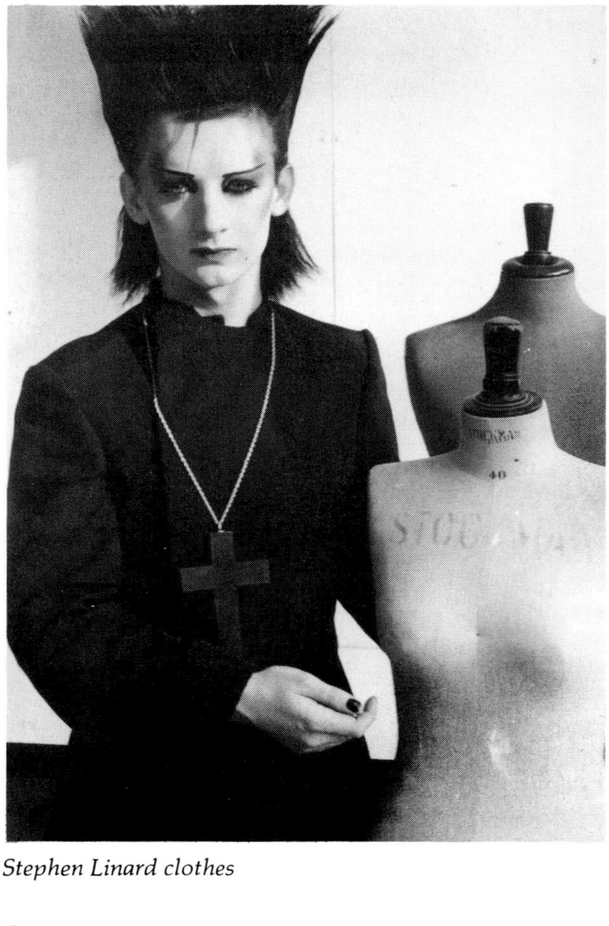

Stephen Linard clothes

Nun George with Stephen Linard, 1980

Mary Magdalen at Hell, 1980

ジョージ

GEORGE:Mode-"I'm a budding celebrity,the immaculate conception".The nuns habi "I made it myself dear".Crucifix-"A present from the Vatican".Kung Fu slipper -£4.99 from a Chinese supermarket.Make up-a mix of Lichner and Biba.Fave musi Marc Bolan,Julie Andrews,Pearl Bailey,The Sweet and Bach.Dislikes-"Lounge - Lizards"and Spandau Ballet.

ith Kirk Brandon

Caught by Perry Haines, 1980

Getting on a coach to Margate, 1980

With Kirk on Margate coach

At the Carburton Street squat in 1980, watching a house on fire: George with Kirk Brandon, Andy Polaris, Jamie Morgan and others

8

レフテナント・ラッシュ

Lieutenant Lush

Malcolm McLaren, former manager of the New York Do the Sex Pistols and BowWowWow, and today als notable performer in his own right, is rarely short of a sche or two. So when the word went round that McLaren wan different people to try out singing some jazz songs at Rainbow theatre in Finsbury Park, no-one was surprised.

For George, it was a suitable opportunity to have a go but when he went there, events took an unexpected turn. N he believes McLaren was displeased with Annabell performance as lead singer with BowWowWow and wanted frighten her a bit: "At the time I thought he was doing m favour, but actually he was doing himself a favour."

Whatever McLaren's motivation, Boy George brie became Lieutenant Lush — joint vocalist with Annabella BowWowWow. He did several gigs with them, including o at the Rainbow and one in Manchester, and received go notices in the music press. But a planned national tour w called off and the relationship between George and McLar deteriorated, so he decided to sever his connections and try form his own band.

"One thing I want to stress quite adamantly is th Malcolm McLaren never had anything to do with Cultu Club," he stresses now. "He didn't even want me BowWowWow, Matthew (Ashman, guitarist) wanted me BowWowWow. Malcolm thought I was a stupid new romant so it's not like I'm one of his protégés."

Annabella and George. He's the big one.

Malcolm Mc

FRP: What do you think about George getting to number one?

MM: I'm glad. I like George. I think he's very sexy and I think he's amusing and intelligent. He really has a great voice. I just hope he sings better songs. I think George is good, I always have. I remember when I put him into BowWowWow, the reason why I did it was because Annabella was too much of a problem, she was a good idea and that's terrible.

I realise that the one major mistake that I ever made, is that you can't sell ideas, what you can do, is sell people. Ideas are too abstract. BowWowWow was an idea. George was a person, he had a thing of his own. Annabella didn't have anything. She'd just watched Top of the Pops for a year before I met her and that was the sum total of her experience except for an odd Stevie Wonder album. It was very difficult you see, and however much I tried to model and so on, eventually I realised that that was just stupid

Mother's boy

Annabella

Q. What about the rumour that you were supposed to be getting kicked out of Bow Wow Wow?

A. I wonder who started that. It was probably due to the fact that we had this guy . . . you know, we've made the show a bit bigger: we've got two dancers instead of having the old fashioned idea of just having a singer and a group. It's got more action now. It's such a dancey kind of music, and we needed some action in it and wanted to liven it up a bit. So we got some dancers and this guy George to do a couple of songs. I don't really know him that well yet, but he's okay. He used to be at Blitz a lot.

Q. What does your mum think to all this?

A. She's very happy for me.

THIS terrifying apparition on the right is George O'Dowd, sometime singer with Bow Wow Wow (until manager Malcolm McLaren fired him) and now leader of a new band called Culture Club.

George's problem is that everyone thinks he's a girl.

"My mother wouldn't like that," pouts George, 20. "But when I went on stage during a gig with the Bow Wows in Manchester everyone thought I was Annabella (the 15-year-old lead singer) and the boys were grabbing at me.

"I really don't dress up as a woman—I just like looking feminine."

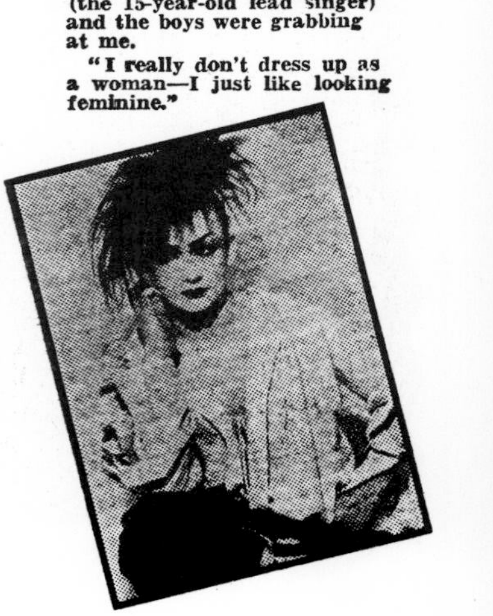

ROLE MODELS

Put a couple of punks together with a skinhead, a ted and a New Romantic and you might expect a riot. But all's peace when the motive is profit. This motley lot are the latest models on the books of the Peter Benison agency – models with a difference in that they live the parts they play. 'It's our new weirdo side,' says Gabriella who handles their bookings. 'But they have to be reliable, honest, clean – and with good skin.' Before Benison stepped in, claims Gabriella, oddities like these were picked up in the street or at clubs by advertising art directors, and paid a pittance for their work. Now they'll have proper contracts. Left to right: George, a window-dresser who has posed for the Trustee Savings Bank; Dave, who despite his good skin has yet to get a booking; Jordan, who's also an actress; hairdresser James, who's been seen munching in a Sara Lee cake ad; and Sue, a technical artist, who has been used to boost British Airways. Move over, Jerry Hall?

At this point, George's career took a turn that led
ntually to the legendary Foundry clothing range. When the
yal Shakespeare Company desperately needed an "authentic
ık look" for their production of *Naked Robots*, George's
loubted talents as a stylist were recommended to them by
friend Mad Jean. The job led him to Street Theatre, a
tume clothes shop in Newburgh Street, where he bribed
s Peter Small into providing free costumes in return for a
ntion in the RSC programme. Peter liked George's sense of
le and after the RSC job, when George was short of cash, he
him to work as a window-dresser.

Another of Peter Small's talented young associates was
igner Sue Clowes. George had thought little of the dress
igns she had brought in, but one day she produced some
ric print ties that greatly impressed him. They combined
ir talents to produce imaginative clothing ideas and Peter
them up in a separate shop, The Foundry, around the corner
Ganton Street.

Shortly after the BowWowWow episode, EMI's Ashley
odall tried to persuade him to become a solo artist but
orge, brought up in a large, volatile but close-knit family and
ays needing the tension of working with people who are
se to him, was never inspired by this idea.

"They didn't even know I could sing. I'd just be a product
l I didn't fancy that."

George set his mind on forming a band . . . but where was
to find the right people?

DAILY STAR, Thursday, May 29, 1980

WEIRDIES!

Mirror Woman

FLAMBOYANT: George O'Dowd, 19, wears Chinese slippers (£3.99), old school trousers he tapered himself, and leg warmers. A black crepe Twenties dress—20p from Oxfam—is pinned round his waist. Various tassle belts were picked up for a few pence, as were the long scarf and Oxfam beads round his neck. He got the wooden cross from a friend, the crimplene blouse from his mum. A black felt hat and assorted earrings round off the outfit.

PAR
DO-I

THE kids on t
of the page a
new Romantic
they're dressing up to
in an outlandish fa
movement sweeping B

They have a passion
romantic eras of bygone d
their style is bizarr
extravagant.

Anything goes as long
over the top and helps th
out a pantomime fantasy
past.

They dress the same swa
way as the new breed of ro
such as Adam and the A
Steve Strange of Visage.

And now they're leading
Paris fashion houses by th

For it's the street fashi
ated by the new Romanti
dominated last week's Par
ion shows.

Name your favourite c
drama and it was bound t
been represented there by
look" for next autumn.

Show upon show, ther
were—the tartan Bonnie

LO

FLASHY: Fashion student S
Hanson wears one of her
creations. Her favourite peri
history is the eighteenth ce
and her outfit—organza d
with silk taffeta vest and pa
loons—reflects the glory of
bygone era.

George and Jeremy

Photo by Kate Fantayzee

orge window-dressing at the Regal in Newburgh Street,
o owned by Street Theatre's Peter Small

Early Foundry sessions, 1982

9

ドクター・バレンタイン

Dr Valentine

Michael Emile Craig was born less than half a mile from Hammersmith Odeon — in what is still his family home today — on February 15th, 1960. He has four sisters and two brothers, one of whom — Greg — is percussionist with Funkapolitan.

Mikey's father toured his native Jamaica as a singer with various bands before coming over to fight in the war. Afterwards he decided to stay in Britain, where he was joined by his wife. His experiences on the English pub circuit gave him a good insight into the difficulties of a performer's life,

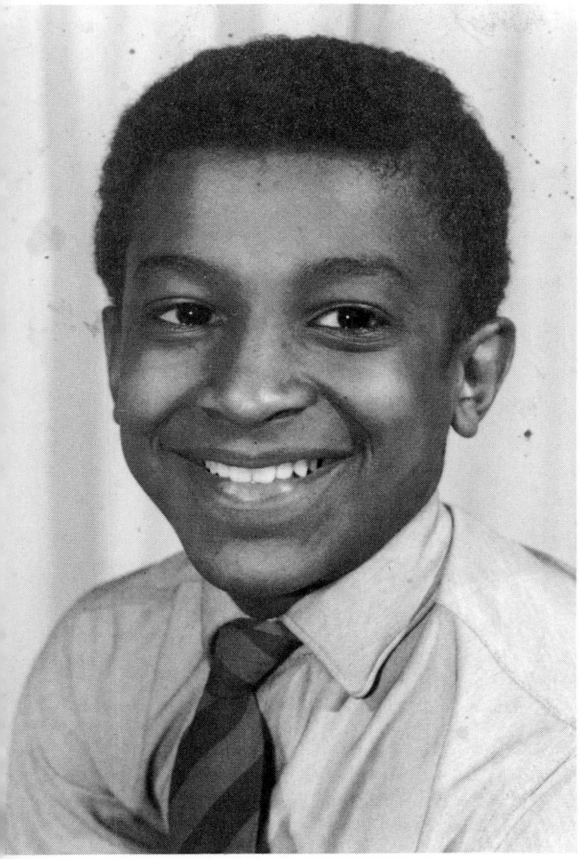

and for a long time he was firmly set against any notion of Mikey becoming a professional musician.

It was a strict and respectable working-class environment in which the Craig children were raised. Good manners and academic achievement rated highly; Mikey, it was hoped, would one day join a good, secure profession — as a doctor, or a lawyer, a pilot perhaps.

But there were a few years grace before such weighty matters came to the fore. "The first thing that ever hit me, when I was five, was The Monkees," Mikey remembers. "I was crazy about The Monkees and my father used to take me to Woolworths every weekend to buy Monkees records. I had every record they ever released. We had this massive collection of 60s hits here and then, come the 70s, he starts laying down this academic trip."

The first two years at a boys' grammar school in Shepherds Bush were promising enough — though mainly, as it turned out, because of the charisma of an English teacher by the name of Dr Valentine. "He was superb," says Mikey. "While he was at the school I was always near the top of the class in English, because during his lessons I was just absorbed by him. I don't know what was causing it, but he seemed to magnetise me when he was working, so whatever he was explaining soaked right in. Then he left and I just went *pshhhhht* — straight down. I can't forget his face though."

The atmosphere at school was not such as to make for any lasting friendships — "There were hardly any blacks at all, and you had to be more or less white yourself; the friends I had at school were just fair-weather friends" — and the only school activity he really enjoyed was sport. He played football for the school and the borough, but when he was asked to do trials for Fulham and Brentford Football Clubs, his parents wouldn't let him: "They wanted academics first, so they wouldn't sign the papers."

カメラがクレージー

10

ザ・ホワイト・ハウス

the white house

efore long, Mikey started looking elsewhere for things to keep him occupied.

"I was fully grown when I was about 13, so I could just mper around and go into pubs and things. After Dr entine left I had nothing to look forward to at school and I rted to go to Ronnie Scott's and various other clubs in ek Street and Wardour Street. I used to dance a hell of a Dancing was important to us as kids. Everyone was ling to be the best."

When he was 15, he developed a strange fascination a white Georgian house close to his own home, looking at very time he walked by. One day, a friend called Trevor ed to say he'd been kicked out of his house and was now ying with Erin Pizzey (the writer and organiser of homes battered women) who was a friend of his. He invited key to come round.

That phone call had a profound influence on the rest Mikey's life. Erin Pizzey, it turned out, lived in the house that had fascinated him so much. She also had a daughter named Cleo who became Mikey's girlfriend.

The dance floor gave way to the turntables as Mikey became DJ at Club Sept in Soho. The music he played and listened to was mainly uptempo gay disco and funk.

"But I got very frustrated about sitting behind turntables," he recalls. "I wanted to be actually playing, because I'm a very physical kind of person. I need to *do* the thing. And then a friend of mine brought a bass guitar round under mysterious circumstances. . . I don't know where it came from. Anyway, I've always liked the sound of the bass guitar — sometimes it's the anchor and sometimes it runs off into a little melody and comes back to its roots again. So I started to learn off records — Bob Marley records, *Exodus* and things like that, and one or two funkyish records, *A Taste of Honey* — things that had certain styles, so I could trace them."

He was now living with Cleo in a flat, and they had their first child, a boy named Kito. To provide the money they desperately needed, Mikey took on a number of outdoor jobs, such as roadbuilding, before deciding that was too cold. He found himself a job in a sound studio. "I started off as a tape op, hoping to work my way up. I was quite good at it, editing and things like that," he says.

His guitar vanished as mysteriously as it had arrived. "The guy came back and said, I need some money and I need it back, I'm gonna go and sell it. I was most upset but I didn't know whose it was. It wasn't mine. So I gave it back to him."

But by now he was firmly hooked. He bought himself a new bass guitar and started jamming with friends.

Cleo gave birth to their second child Amber, a girl. The pressures and responsibilities they faced were really too great to make for a stable and happy life; six months after Amber was born, Cleo decided to go and live in Bristol, where Erin had another house. At first, Mikey stayed in London, "but, longing to see the kids, I followed her about three weeks afterwards and we lived down there for about two years."

Mikey was 18 when he moved to Bristol, and while there he firmly decided that working in studios was no more his scene than working on the roads: he wanted to form a band. It was hard to make progress in Bristol. He played with various people there — "they were mainly older than me, long-haired hippies but very good musicians" — but grew increasingly frustrated at the lack of opportunity. Eventually he persuaded Cleo to move back to London with him, and they lived in a flat in Erin Pizzey's house.

Some eight months later he was still looking around until one day he picked up the NME and saw a picture of George and Annabella, with a story that suggested Malcolm McLaren might want to form a separate band with George.

"I knew some people who work for Malcolm at World's End, so I phoned them and asked if there was any truth in the rumour. This friend of mine said, well, Malcolm says things like this and never carries them through. So I said, well, I'd like to carry it through, so could you introduce me to this George guy?"

With Jeremy Fantayzee, 1980

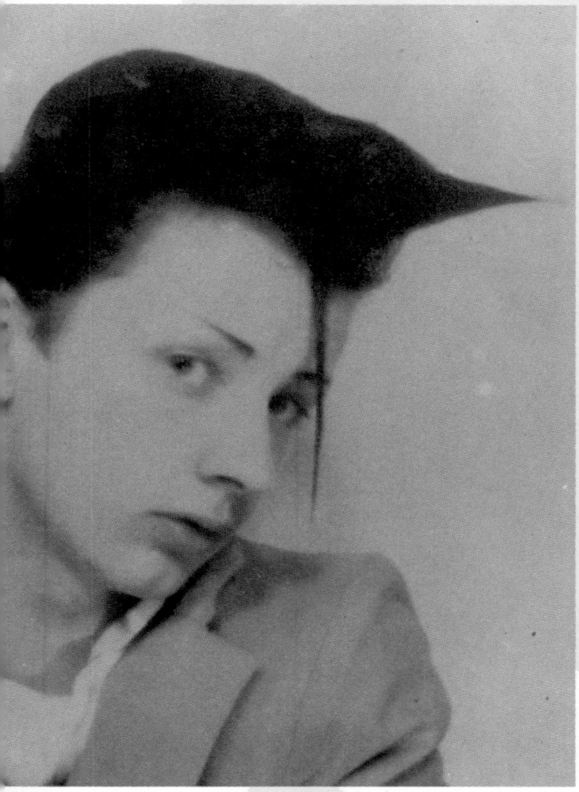

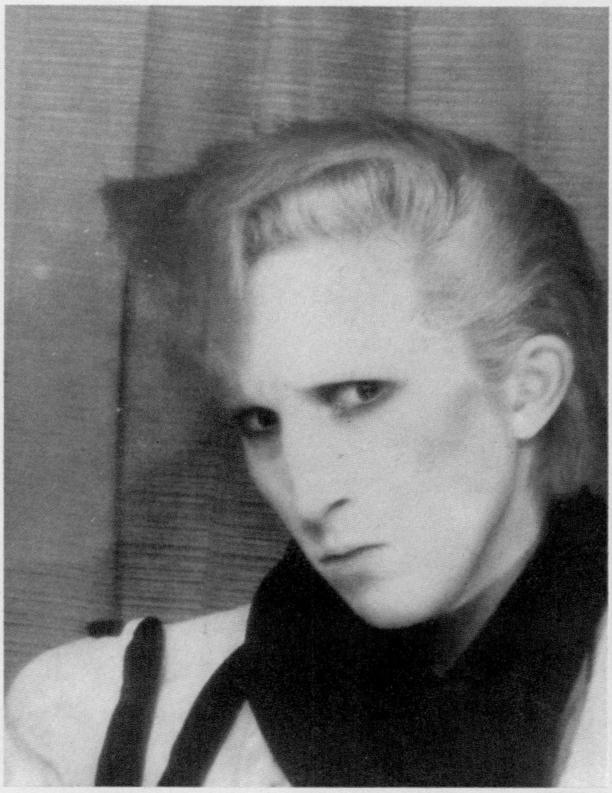

Martin Degville

Medusa Boy

KULTUR

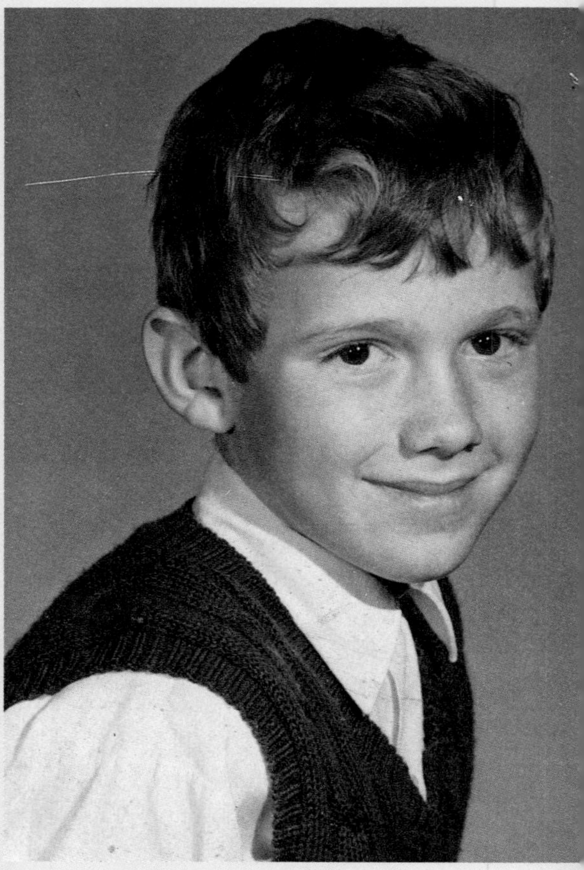

MIKEY

ROY

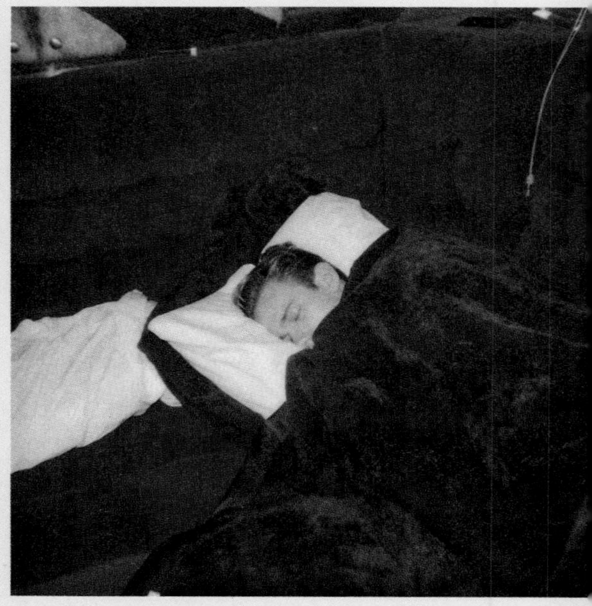

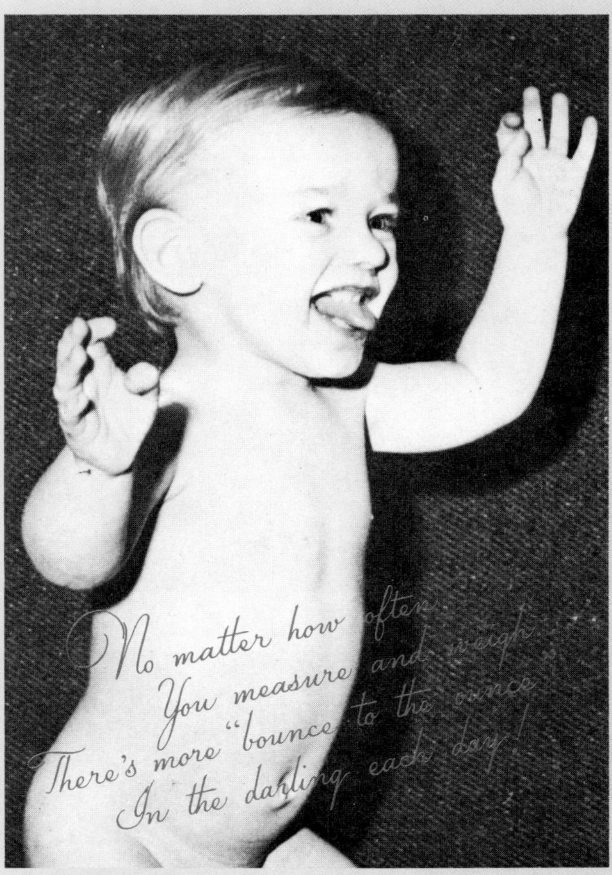

JON

BOY

George with birthday presents, June 14, 1983

With Patti Bell

With Paranoid Pete

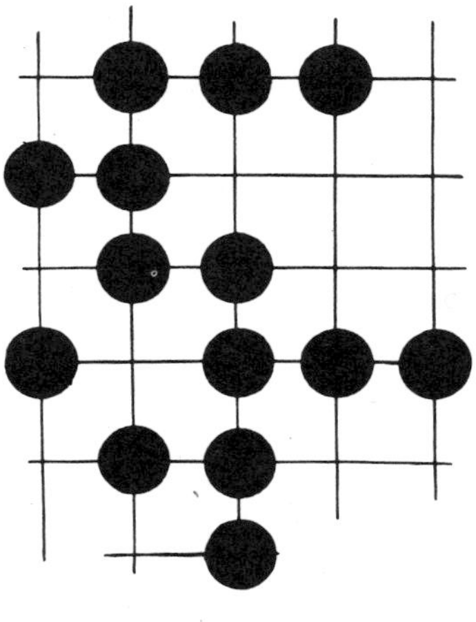

With Jo

Kissing to be clever

'ith Babs

With Andy Polaris — "ebony and ivory"

"My Marlene Dietrich look"

ボーイ・ジョージ

t Le Kilt, 1980

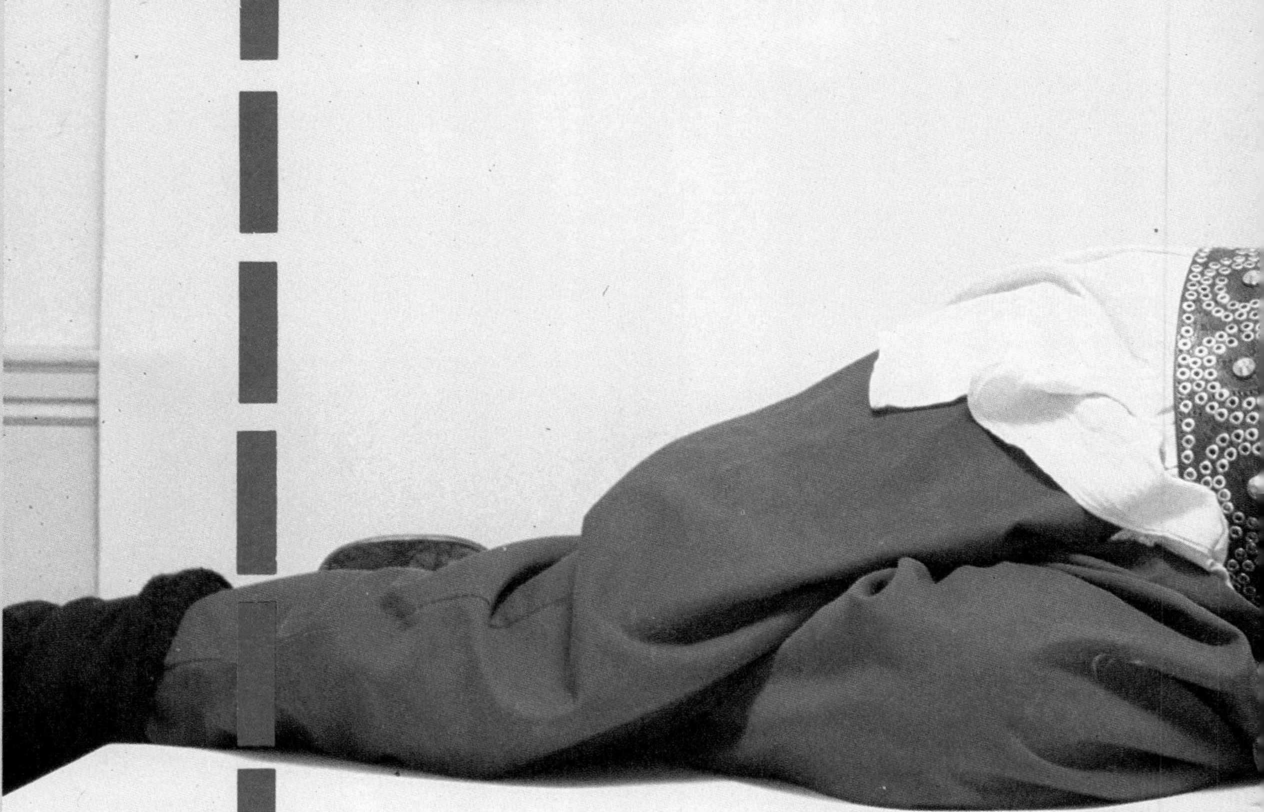

→ TO GEORGE →
PEACE + LOVE
MIYO
Boy George O'Dowd
ESPECIA
FOR YOU ON
VALENTINE DAY
Boy
george
Boy:-
GEORGE
To Boy George
from Natasha
aged 6
I love you
Tom
Tim
John
Bill
Jack
dick
harry
arthur
Can you tick your name off please
Boy George
Culture Club

CULTURE CLUB
BRISTOL
R 9
COLSTON HALL
CULTURE CLUB
SUNDAY MAR. 27th
EVENING 7.30 PM
£4.50
STALLS
To

GEORGIE-BOY
BOY GEORGE
BY Rachel
Boy George
CULTURE CLUB

Boy George
Boy George
of
Culture
Club

CULTURE
CLUB
BOY
GEORGE
Boy George

NIGHTLIFE 2
OR NON NIGHT LIFE
GEORGE AND JON ARE SENSIBLE AND HAVE AN EARLY NIGHT (APPARENTLY)
GEORGE'S SIDE
George
To George
Best Wishes
Tom Johnston
NIGHTLIFE
BLOODY ENGLISH POP GROUPS
OH! BUT IM A GREAT CULTURE CLUB FAN!
DO YOU REALLY WANT TO HURT ME
PINOCCHIO GEORGE
HIROMI
MIKEY
Culture Club
One Thursday night.....
IT'S A GIRL
NO, ITS A BOY
YEAH, IT IS
LOOK BOY GEORGE
5.
AT SCHOOL
I REALLY LIKE BOY GEORGE
... love from

11

ア・カルチュラル シング

a cultural thing

In the winter of 1956, a Jewish girl from Middlesbrough, then living in the London district of Wandsworth, had a liaison with a professional violinist.

On September 11th, 1957, she duly gave birth to a baby son. Unable to look after him, she had him adopted by the Moss family, who named him Jonathan Aubrey and raised him in a caring environment.

Jon came to love his adoptive parents as his own. The family observed major Jewish feasts like Passover, the Jewish New Year and Yom Kippur, but they ate bacon and paid little regard to the ritual of Friday nights: Jewishness was regarded as a cultural rather than a religious thing. Nonetheless, Jon's parents felt he ought to make his own choice, and to enable him to do so they sent him to Sunday school at the synagogue from the age of five.

"I went along and it was horrible," he remembers now. "There were all these kids talking about lighting the candles, and I didn't know anything about it. I really didn't want to know. Everybody has their own way but, for me, I don't think religion is the way to God. But Jewish culture is amazing — it's intellectual, always questioning."

The schools he went to were all strict Church of England. At the first school, he recalls, the headmistress had a long leather whip to discipline the kids. "Some of these schools are a bit out of order, you know what I mean? When you left school, the boys had to bow and the girls had to curtsy — it was really Victorian. I used to think it was a load of cobblers, but you still do it."

At this school he met his closest childhood friend — Mike Morris, who now works at the Institute of Contemporary Arts and was involved in organising a recent Laurie Anderson tour.

It soon became apparent that Jon was small for his age, so his father told him he'd have to learn how to fight. He started boxing at the age of five and stayed with it till he was 15, fighting in school competitions. He was considered a promisi young fighter, and his trainers wanted him to c tinue. "But I didn't want to do it. Getting knock about like that, it's not good for you. I'd be finish now, because I'd have been boxing for nearly years. It isn't a good game . . . It's bad for y brain."

His first involvement with music was playi pop tunes by ear on the piano, but he resisted parents' suggestions to take lessons; when he return to music, at the age of 14, he followed brother's example and opted for drums.

By this time he was at Highgate, a pub school in London, where he didn't cut his hair five years and was interested mainly in sports. the academic side he did well in the arts, disastrously elsewhere. "I failed my maths O-le six times. I don't know what was the matter w me, because I'm quite a logical person, but I ne understood it."

After his O-levels (he bagged four) his fat suggested he start working straightaway, but insisted he wanted to stay at school for his A-lev

"The two years I had after my O-levels w really good," he remembers. He learned to en reading and promoted several pop concerts.

His musical activity had remained a const factor in the background; regular practice sessic took place with his brother and a friend called N Feldman, who is now in Huang Chung. His fluences were wide-ranging: "I used to like Ba Ryan, The Beatles, The Searchers and Freddie A The Dreamers. When I was 13, I used to listen to a of jazz. In the 70s there was a big gap in music — p

sic was paperlace and white planes and I didn't
lly like that, so I listened to King Crimson, the
ppelin albums, Wizzard. I really liked Spirit,
nes Taylor, Sly And The Family Stone and a load
New York session musicians who had a band
ed Ripple. I didn't really have any taste, which
s good because I was always openminded. I
nt to see Average White Band and there were 50
ople there."

Jon rounded off his school career with a
ditable result: three A-levels, in English, Politics
d History.

nel and Audrey Moss with Jon and David

with Mum and brother David

12

ティンカー・テイラー

tinker tailor

After school Jon first joined his father in the rag trade, at a big clothing store at Cambridge Circus, on the site now occupied by Wendy Hamburgers. It didn't last long: after two months, eager to make his own way, he walked out.

He got off to an auspicious start when he joined the Marquee Studios as a tape op. "It was terrible," he recalls. "On my first day there the guy said, set up a session for an orchestra — and I didn't know what he was talking about. And he came in and the orchestra were all there and nothing was set up. So he hit me — because at that time I was a bit frail, a bit pretty- looking, you know."

Jon's parents, though allowing him to live at home, gave him to understand that he would get no financial support: if he was determined to make his own way, he had to rely on himself. It was a good lesson, but at first a hard one. At the Marquee, he was earning £16 a week — and even in the mid-70s that didn't go very far when you had to eat out most of the time.

The job soon became unbearable, and for a while Jon tried his hand at salesmanship. It wasn't his strongest quality. "I went to work for this brilliant guy, who made the best cakes I've ever eaten in my life. I literally went round the streets with a paper bag and pulled out the cake and said, what about this then? I didn't sell one cake in a month, not one. He was paying me £10 a week and at the end of the month he said, look, I can't afford to pay you. And I said, well, I've got to go, so I left."

He hated a brief spell as apprentice printer and, after a six-month period as van-driver, he gained his first real experience of the music business when he joined an agency run by Bob England, now manager of The Darts, and Paul King, now manager of Tears For Fears. It was the first job he really enjoyed, but like the others it was shortlived. "One night we went and saw The Darts, and the next I knew the agency had closed and they'd all pissed off."

13

ロックンロール

rock 'n' roll

Jon's earliest attempt at a band was Phone Bone Boulevard, an outfit he set up with Nick Feldman. The only noteworthy event that occurred with this band was that Thomas Dolby played a gig with them once.

Then, when they "suddenly realised" they were all Jewish, they changed the name to Pastrami Barmy. "We made this album cover with a rabbi, with a big thing of bacon in front of him, pulling his hair out. Because pastrami is like, Jewish ham, you know . . ."

Briefly they became Eskimo Norbert — "pathetic, you know, but some good ideas."

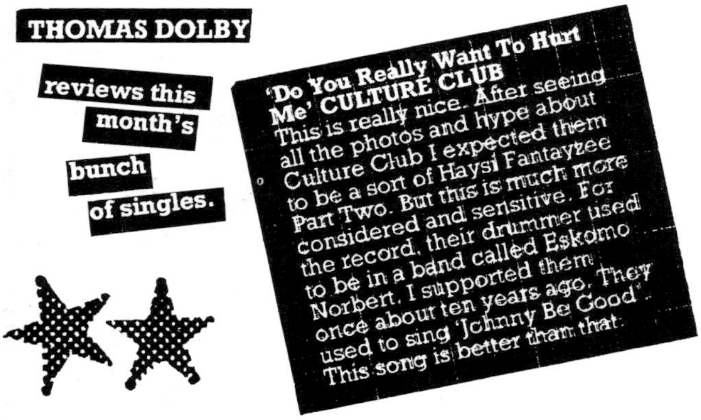
THOMAS DOLBY

reviews this month's bunch of singles.

'Do You Really Want To Hurt Me' CULTURE CLUB
This is really nice. After seeing all the photos and hype about Culture Club I expected them to be a sort of Haysi Fantayzee Part Two. But this is much more considered and sensitive. For the record, their drummer used to be in a band called Eskomo Norbert. I supported them once about ten years ago. They used to sing 'Johnny Be Good'. This song is better than that.

When Bob England's agency vanished overnight, Jon became more determined than ever to join a 'proper' band.

"This is when punk rock was starting," he says. "The first time I saw the Sex Pistols I thought, what a load of wankers, I hated them. But after a month I just thought they were brilliant."

He regularly checked the music press for suitable ads; then one day found a likely one that said, 'Drummer Wanted'.

"So I went there, it was in Camden Town. And this really little bloke met me — glasses, short hair, leather jacket, pink brothel creepers. It was Bernie Rhodes.

"I went in and Joe Strummer was there. the wall it had The Clash, but I didn't really kn who they were.

"Strummer said, oh, you don't look v good, your hair is too fucking long, and all th And I said, what band are you? He says, I'm r telling you, we'll have to try you out — it was all t bollocks, you know, like the Boys' Own m Anyway, I played the drums and they w impressed.

"And I said, you're The Clash, aren't you? said, how do you know? So I said, it's on your ba man, you've got it on the back of your jacket. He j said, fuck off.

"So they asked me back and I decided to g my hair cut. And that night when I got my hair cu got beaten up really badly.

"So I thought, this has got to be good, this h to be the start. Everything had gone wrong - didn't have a job, I didn't have a girlfriend, r parents hated me, I'd been beaten up and I had t stupid haircut.

"So I went back and joined The Clash."

Jon's career with The Clash lasted ab two months. He joined them when they had ju recorded **White Riot**, with Terry Jones on drun and they got their deal with CBS while he was w them. But the mix of personalities didn't work; th attitudes were too different.

"I used to have rows with Mick Jones a also with Bernie, although Bernie and I got on ve well in a funny sort of way. But I just didn't agr with everything and, being in The Clash, you had believe in what they were doing. All strength them, they really did believe it at the time. But I do want to do it and there was no sense of humo which I really didn't like."

He left The Clash and phoned up Riff Regar "the funniest bloke I've ever met" — who wanted form a band. Together with Steve Royce th formed London and within a week — with a little of help from Simon Napier Bell — they'd signed deal with MCA and were on tour with T Stranglers. Jon's first tour was a baptism by fire - lasted six weeks, every day without a break.

But London collapsed — largely, Jon n thinks, because they took themselves t seriously.

Rat Scabies had just left The Damned a they were looking for a drummer. Jon knew t Brian James had a particular liking for the Iggy The Stooges album, so before auditioning listened to it carefully.

"And when I went there he played this Ig number, and I thought, great, I know it. So I play everything perfectly and they said, yeah, all righ

playing drums with Eskimo Norbert

He had two days rehearsal to learn two albums, then went on the road again. "It was really good fun then, because it was **bang bang bang bang**, action all the time. The only trouble was that it was really rock'n'roll — it was fighting and beer on your head and a lot of speed, booze, drugs. At that time I was really into it. I used to wear all black. And I lost a stone."

On New Year's Eve, 1977, Jon set out to go and see The Ramones; he never got there. A bad car crash on the way put him in hospital for ten days.

"Nobody from the band came to see me," he recalls. "It was a bit like that, you know, nobody gives a shit. But all the Stranglers came to see me — that was really nice."

But The Damned were not destined to last. Their popularity dropped sharply after Rat Scabies left. "He was a brilliant showman, that guy. I could match his playing — that bit was easy — but not his showmanship. And the big snowball just melted in the end."

14

ザ・エッジ アンド・ビヨンド

The Edge and beyond

When The Damned broke up, Jon teamed up with guitarist Lu and together they disappeared to Lu's home village in Norfolk.

"It was this tiny village, really manic. Everybody gets pissed and they get off with each other's wives and do nothing — a really unblack sort of place; it had no soul in it at all.

"So we went up there and he'd built this studio with his bare hands, a big room. He'd dug the foundations, put concrete in and then covered it with egg boxes. It was a proper studio, with glass and everything, and a little four-track. Amazing."

They called themselves The Edge — "a forerunner to the Theatre of Hate, Sex Gang Children sort of thing that's going on now, but the musicianship was better" — and wrote enough material to fill about three albums in four weeks.

After their retreat, they rehearsed in London in a derelict house owned by a tolerant dentist a occupied mostly by a large number of motorbik and their owners. A party at this house was t occasion for meeting Kirk Brandon, a contact w was to play an important part later on.

In the end, The Edge became a stable backi band as Jane Ayre And The Belvederes, and J lost interest. It was time for another rethink.

"I had no money, no band, I'd left my girlfrie — I had nothing. I had to go back to my paren They thought I was an idiot, I was just staring at t wall for three months. I didn't know what to do."

He blew his last £250 on a weekend Exegesis training. "It was all — 'You're a wank what are you?', 'I'm a wanker' . . . a positive thinki weekend. All my friends had done it and I'd be saying that they were idiots, but in the en thought, what the hell. So I went along and ga them the £250. I knew they were ripping me off, b I didn't care. I did this weekend thing and I we mad, I thought I could change the colour of traf lights . . ."

One day he received a call from his e girlfriend, who told him Adam Ant had left his ba and wanted him to play drums. "So I went to me Adam and Marco. It was weird — he was rea quiet and intense. He said, I've got this idea for tw drummers, and he put this tape on with the Burun stuff. I said okay, great."

He didn't hear anything for two weeks a then received a phone call summoning him Rockfield, Wales. He put his drums in the back of h estate car, drove straight down there and record **Kick** and **Cartrouble**, putting one drumbeat on t of another. The engineer was Chris Hughes, no one of Adam's drummers and his producer.

"And that was it — I just got a session fee don't really care about the money, because th wasn't the point. I didn't really show mu enthusiasm and Adam could see that, so that w the end of that. And then he got to Number O about six months later . . ."

Jon never really regretted that his encount with Adam didn't last. What he wanted was a ba in which he could make his own, origi contribution, and for a drummer that's not alwa easy to find.

"Then one day the phone rang and this gu went, '**bababababababa** . . .' He said, '**we-wan a-drummer-but-we-don't-want-you-but-w might-want-you-if-you're-right-so-can-yo come-down-but-it-doesn't-mean-you're-i the-band-right?**' I said, yeah, yeah, all right, ha on. And he said, '**I-used-to-be-in-BowWowWo - but-I'm-too-effeminate-they-think-I'm-a-b of-a-poof-and-everything-but-you-know-yo can-come-down**' . . ."

15

ギター・ヒーロー

guitar hero

Roy Ernest Hay was born in Southend on August 12th, 1961, the second son in a respectable ckers' family. "Ernest is my mother's fault," he nfides. "She had a great-uncle named Ernest and s made me suffer ever since."

After a spell at nearby Canvey, the family moved their present home in Corringham, close to sildon, Essex. Roy lived there until 1981.

He received his education at a comprehensive school near Basildon and enjoyed maths, arts and music. "I've always been into music since daddy forced me into piano lessons when I was a kid."

Roy was never a real 'record-buying kid' — "I didn't go out and buy ten singles every week or anything. I think the first record I ever bought was the New Seekers, then 10CC. And I used to like Marmalade. My older brother was a rock fan and I went through that phase for quite a few years. I listened to Yes and Genesis, and Led Zeppelin. I still listen to them occasionally now — it's good to listen to."

Discovering the guitar at 15, he became a guitar hero for two years — "you know, learning all the solos and trying to beat every other guitarist in the area."

He left school at 16 with no specific idea of what he wanted to do. He had no desire to continue at school and try to get to university, so he took what seemed to be the only other option — a job at an insurance office in London. There he made friends with a fellow victim, Keith Giddons.

"I did it for about three years, but halfway through I began to get bored and tried to think of a career. A friend of mine was a hairdresser and I thought, well, he seems to be having a good time, so I decided to go for that."

At 19, he found he had to swallow his pride a bit at the hair salon in Stamford, Essex — taking instructions from a girl three years his junior. "But after a while," he remembers, "I started taking on a bit more responsibility and it was fun."

He'd kept up his involvement in music, at one time changing back and forth between piano and guitar, unable to choose between the two. Borrowing a drumkit to put down the beat, he made some Joy Division-inspired demo tapes at home and by this method learned much about the structure of songs and music. In June 1981 he met Alison Green at Crocs nightclub in Rayleigh. He fell in love with Alison and became guitarist in her brother Robin's band Russian Bouquet.

Back in London, Keith popped into Street Theatre one day, where George mentioned that he was looking for a guitarist.

"Well," said Keith, "I know a guy . . ."

16

ミュージック・フォー マムズ・アンド ベイビー・シスターズ

music for mums and baby sisters

Mikey's friend at World's End said – okay, come along to Planets (a Piccadilly club) in a couple of days' time; and that is how the first meeting between Mikey and George was arranged.

"It's difficult to describe what it was like," says Mikey, "I sensed a lot of power around him, and strength. Not physically, but just the aura he was giving off was positive and I liked that. I said to him, I've read about you in the NME, that Malcolm wants to form a band for you – would you like to get one together? And he said, yeah, I'd like to, but Malcolm won't be involved."

George and Mikey duly formed a band, with a guy called John 'Suede' on guitar. They called it The Sex Gang Children (George later passed the name on to the group now using it), started rehearsing and wrote a song called Mask. Meanwhile, they looked around for a drummer and, on the advice of his friend Kirk Brandon, George phoned Jon Moss.

On the face of it, it was impossible to imagine a more unlikely contact than that between Boy George and Jon Moss. George was London's supreme poseur, and though he always kept his own counsel and was careful not to be considered part and parcel of the Spandau Ballet/Visage scene, there was barely an article about new romantics or Blitz kids in any magazine without at least a photograph of Boy George. Jon, on the other hand, was completely turned off by the Blitz scene – "I just thought it stank. I'm a bit of a puritan at heart, so I suppose I went out of the back door for a while."

But – things being rarely what they seem – the meeting proved to be a crucial stage in moulding together the elements needed for a successful pop group.

For Jon, that first meeting in March 1981 contrasted favourably with other auditions he'd gone in for. He walked in, greeted Kirk, and turned to George. "I just said, hello, and looked at him. He was very down-to-earth. He said, hello – all right? You know what he's like, sort of flirty, coy. I thought, oh, he's nice.

"Mikey was there as well – I remember thinking I liked him, he was very nice, but he used to borrow money and take cigarettes all the time. And John was there – he was a really nice guy.

"I'd brought my drums and started playing. They had this song called Mask, which was horrible. Anyway, I remember thinking, this guy is gr George is like that, everybody really likes him. He can be really nasty, got a very sharp tongue, but on the whole he's very lovable. And whe started singing, I thought – shit song, shit band, brilliant voice.

"The other thing is, he didn't just want me to go BOOMBOOM BOOMBOOMtata. . . He said, what do you want to do? Play somethin the drums. So I played a really African beat, because I was into that at time. And he said, yeah, I like that. So I thought great, I can put input in be creative."

It soon became apparent that Jon's input was not going to be con ed to the musical field alone.

"He was what was needed at the time," says Mikey. "He had m of a business head than me. I'm just into playing music. He's been thro god knows how many bands and he's seen it all before. And he's not m ing a point, you know. He just knows what's best, really."

Thus, some of the functions of each member of the band w already becoming clear at this early stage. The experiences of each them gave them a shared determination to achieve success. In m respects, George is the band's creative powerhouse, with never less t a million or so ideas floating around – and most of them good ones. Mi provided a musical anchor and a broader scope of influences and mo But what they badly needed was professional and musical discipline. S George: "I need somebody to say, right, do this, do that, and let's get with it. And when I met Jon, that's what happened."

The first essential change was the name.

"When George told me it was called The Sex Gang Children, I sa no way man," remembers Jon. A new approach was needed. "I wasn't to the Blitz kids thing. Everything was bleak and cold and I said, look m we need religion, we need warmth, we need colour.

"When George and I talked, I said, look, I've been in loads of bar and I want to be in a commercial band. I want to be in a band that s

Poser meets Puritan: George and Jon

ls of records and that your mother likes. I want my mother to like the sic I'm making and I want my baby sister to like it. I don't care about my nds. I don't care about the 18-21 year olds, because all you're doing is ıg for other people all the time.

"The thing about George is that he didn't need to be all dark and ak, because he's a really happy character. And all our songs are childish way. Do You Really Want To Hurt Me is quite childish, but it's great. got real affection and warmth and that is what George is.

"George will sit here and scream and grab at everything all over the ce and I was saying, right, go – do this, go there. You know, do it. And vorked."

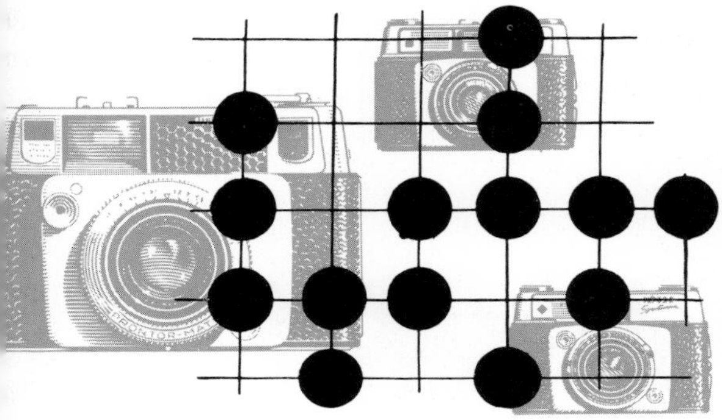

With 'Sister Jenny'

'he first Culture Club line-up: Mikey, George, Jon and uede

17

リシャッフル

reshuffle

Within a few days, the band had written two new songs – The Eyes Of Medusa and I'm An Animal. George was still in contact with EMI, who wanted him to become a solo artist, but he was now firmly set on the notion of developing the band.

"He needs people to work around him," says Mikey, "he needs security and people he can trust. Because at the end of the day, when you get through all that motor mouth, he's a real family type guy. He always talks about his mum and his brothers and his sister and so on. I don't think he could ever be a solo artist."

Nonetheless, the EMI contact was useful. Jon persuaded Ashley Goodall to give the band some studio time to make a demo tape and they recorded their two songs. The result was not convincing, but it gave them good experience and it strengthened Jon's conviction that they needed a new guitarist in place of 'Suede'.

"I just said to George, look, he's got to go and George said, all right, I'll tell him. And about a month passed and nothing happened. Then one day the guy walked into a club, I was really drunk and I just said, I'm really sorry but you're fired."

It wasn't Suede's day. The other three members of the band had all been building up courage to broach the matter with him, and Mikey was under the impression that he told him: "Jon decided this other guitarist wasn't right, which I'd felt before but probably wasn't quite strong enough to tell the guy myself, it's difficult. In the end they left me to tell him, so I told him and he left."

Putting the pieces together, it now seems likely that after a month of dithering, Suede was fired twice on the same day.

They auditioned many guitarists before finding the right one. At Street Theatre, George consulted his customer Keith Giddons. "Then Roy appeared from the suburbs of Rayleigh – you know, real suburban Roy," says Mikey.

Jon recalls that Roy fitted in immediately. "He was brilliant. He wasn't freaked out by me and George, or by Mikey – because Mikey started to get really weird, he had a Mohican and plaits and everything, he looked really good."

Roy was excited by the type of music they were playing, based mainly on guitar-orientated drumbeats and fast vocals. "It was just right," he says. The vibe in the room was good and everyone seemed dedicated to it, which is very important."

He'd heard of George and seen him around the clubs. At the auditi his main impression was amazement at how well George could sing. " sang that old song Private Number. And I thought well, he can defini sing and I've never met anyone who can sing before – it's got to be a g start. Jon impressed me too – his drumming was superb. And Mikey j had the right groove."

Culture Club was now complete. They rehearsed for several mont writing new songs and developing a distinctive image. The first song t wrote with Roy was called Put It Down. "George and I wrote that in flat," Roy explains. "He has always been really into lyrics – he'd jot th down first, play around with them, and then he'd sit down and type th all out. So he sang this lyric and I played around a bit. It was all very vag until we got a drumbeat – we'd write from the drumbeat and just ri basically, and then bang the vocals on top. We must have written ab ten like that, of which we kicked out about eight. I'm Not Crazy w written very much like that, although it's obviously a much refined versi now."

With Paul Raymond's son, George holding the first demo tape (Eyes Of Medusa)

18 ダンシング ライク・クレージー

dancing like crazy

I t was by no means plain sailing from there on. The band had no income and there was a long way to go before they were ready to launch themselves into the public eye.

Roy was still living in Essex (with Alison, who in September 1981 joined Sue and George at The Foundry as an assistant), working as a hairdresser. Three days a week he would catch a train after finishing work at 6pm, rehearse from 8 until about 11, and get home at half past one in the morning. "It was hell," he says. "I think I only ever skipped rehearsals once. It wasn't even fun sometimes, it was just hard work. But you know, you get a feeling about things – you think they're right and it's soon going to happen. And that's the feeling we all had."

Mikey also needed conviction to carry him through the difficult early days. "I don't know exactly what made me carry on, hanging in there

ulture Club at the Holy City Zoo, Birmingham, ovember 1981

doing it. Sometimes it got a bit low, in the early days when we were spending money ourselves and nothing was really happening."

Living in a flat in Erin's house with Cleo and the children wasn't easy: "It was okay, but I always hate living at people's houses because no matter how much they make you feel welcome, they still make you know that it's their place, you know what I mean? I was almost trapped there, to be quite honest with you. But there was nothing I could do – I'd wanted the children as well. Afterwards we realised that maybe it wasn't such a good idea, because we weren't really grown up enough. We did well, but really we should have waited until, like in two years' time maybe I'll have some more money and that would have been a more appropriate time to have children. It makes for a lot of complications. But having said that, I'm really glad they're born. They're really beautiful kids."

George was busy developing the band's image, combining his own ideas with those of Sue Clowes and with Jon's religious notions to produce The Foundry look. Mikey and Cleo's younger brother Amos, among others, were pressed into service as models and colourful, outrageous photosessions started appearing in some of the more enlightened magazines of the day.

At Roy's suggestion, they played their first gig in October 1981 at Crocs, a club in Rayleigh, Essex, that had become famous during the new romantic club boom as the home territory of Depeche Mode.

"The age group there is about 16-22," says Mikey, "and everybody goes out of their way to overdress and get pissed on a Saturday night. You'd find a bunch of rockabillies, a bunch of skinheads probably, a bu of new romantics and Kid Creole lookalikes, all in the same place, wh was really interesting. After the gig I just stood in the corner and looke was amazing. . .some kids were lying flat out on the floor while pe were dancing like crazy around them. It was one hell of a place.

"We were really raucous then. It was just three instrument guitar, drums and bass – and George's voice, all turned up as lou possible to get away with it. We played most of the album then, tho obviously in a different form. It went really well, the kids liked it. T invited us back as well."

Other gigs followed at the Holy City Zoo in Birmingham an Foubert's in London. On Boxing Day 1981 they played their second gi Crocs. In the audience was a chance Christmas visitor to the area by name of Danny Goodwin.

19

キャッシュ
フロム・ケイオス

cash from chaos

By now, Culture Club were actively looking for a record comp deal. One day, while George was working at The Foundry, a walked into the shop and introduced himself as Danny Goodwin, f Virgin Music. He'd seen the band play at Crocs and was excited about t potential. How would they like to do a demo tape?

When they made this tape, they were still some way away from Culture Club sound that finally went public. In the process of learnin sing, George at first tried to sound like all the other singers he liked, the demo was a fairly pale shadow of what they later developed. T recorded I'm Not Crazy, Kissing To Be Clever and Put It Down. Vi Records were not convinced and, for the moment, it was back to drawing board.

"Then it just clicked one day," says George. "I thought, fuck i want to sound like myself."

They also needed to tighten up on arrangements and production, Tony Gordon, who by this time was already becoming quite involved w them and who eventually became their manager, suggested to Jon t they use a producer for the next demo recording. The band agreed, Tony recruited Steve Levine.

For their next move, they revived the EMI connection and recor two tracks – White Boy and I'm Afraid Of Me. "And that came out re d," remembers George. "My voice started developing then."

Interest was expressed by several major companies, but George and were not impressed by what they had to offer.

"When you go into a major record company," says Jon, "it's really ersonal. We went to one and we were introduced to the press artment – 'This is Boy George and Jon Moss from Culture Club,' and sort of went, oh yeah, and carried on with what they were doing. The e is massive and it's all doors. In the big record companies they're all in es and nobody really knows what's going on. Some people never go other departments."

"Their attitude stank," says George succinctly. "It was, like, we can you money, we just want you so we can make a quick buck…"

Virgin Records re-entered the arena and, to Culture Club, this npany seemed much more suited. "It's all open-plan and they all shout ach other," says Jon, "so everyone knows what's going on. It looks chaos…it's cash from chaos and it really works, they've got a very d system. And you have to be very careful, because it can be terrible if haven't got control over what you're doing. Especially for us. If we e marketed in the wrong way, we could look really stupid."

Culture Club now knew exactly what they wanted: a company that e them the freedom to develop in their own way, and that was strong arketing commercial pop records. In the end, these factors proved e important than the detailed financial arrangements, as they were red other deals that on paper seemed better.

BBC tv

BRITISH BROADCASTING CORPORATION
TELEVISION CENTRE WOOD LANE LONDON W12 7RJ
TELEPHONE 01-743 8000 TELEX: 265781
TELEGRAMS AND CABLES: TELECASTS LONDON TELEX

Room AG01
Ext 2036

Dear George,
Many thanks for taking the trouble to supply us with material on your band 'Culture Club'. However, after careful consideration it was our feeling that the group wouldn't be right for the program.

Best of luck and much success for the future, and again thanks.

Yours Sincerely

David Croft

David Croft

(Assistant Producer)
'Riverside'

"Jon and Tony (Gordon) have this great attitude," explains George. "They say, you shouldn't be greedy. Give away things – you have to give to get. We don't need to act like sharp little businessmen. I know my own affairs – I've got it quite well taped."

"On the face of it," says Jon, "Virgin weren't offering as good a deal as the majors. But they were good, they understood. And we can basically do what we like with them. We could have got a bigger advance and better points, but it wouldn't have been as good because we wouldn't have done as well. I'd rather take 75% of a million than 100% of fuck all. So we signed with Virgin."

20

キャプテン クルーシャル

Captain Crucial

Bands fail or succeed on their merits; but the merits needed for commercial success are by no means confined to music alone. Judgment, determination, management and timing can be equally important factors. The relationship you develop with a record company is a matter of great concern.

"You've got to know what you want," Jon points out. "To go to a record company and say, will you give us a deal, is wrong. You go there and say, this is what I want. And you ask ridiculous things and of course they knock you down. And you say, I want this record to be the single – because as soon as you say you're not sure, they'll say, well, I think this one, and somebody else will say, I think that one and then you don't know. You've got to be very strong."

When Culture Club first joined Virgin Records, they needed to assert their own approach. The prevailing custom among new pop bands was still to play exclusive shows and spread the word through the alternative club scene. Virgin could therefore be forgiven for expecting the same approach from their new signing.

"When I went in," says Jon, "they said, what are you going to do with the band? Are you going to play little clubs? I said no. So they said, are you going to play secret gigs? I said no. They said, well, what's going on? So I said, we're just going to go out and do short tours."

They played a series of dates. "Our opening gig at Keele University was good," remembers Mikey, "mainly because the audience was a bit pissed and it was a ball. The power went, actually, during I'll Tumble 4 Ya – the lights went, the sound went, everything. It lasted for a minute or two and then it all came back on again."

The black-out didn't dampen the spirits at Keele, but a dry-up further north at Glasgow was less well received. "It was a disaster," says Mikey. "After four numbers George just turned round and said he wouldn't sing anymore, his voice had gone. So we left the stage and sent somebody out to make an apology and ask people to hang on to their tickets and we'd come back and play a free gig for them. Which we did."

Their first tour ended at Heaven, a club under the arches of Charing Cross, where they were well received by a full house.

Although the first two singles failed to make an impact on the charts, the new opportunities for recording did enable George to develop his idea of bringing in guest musicians for particular songs. This had started when they did the last demo for EMI, which saw the introduction of Captain Crucial, aka Amos, Cleo's younger brother. His toasting proved highly successful, particularly on *Love Twist*.

Roy wasn't so sure at first about involving other musicians. "I wasn't really into the idea at first, I thought, god, what's he doing, you know – a 14-year-old kid. But once I heard that toast, I just knew it was right. We just knew then that it was another good idea."

It was the beginning of what has rapidly become a tradition in Culture Club.

"George wanted a talk-over on the B-side of *Do You Really War Hurt Me?* and I'd known this guy Weasel for quite a while as a s system operator in Ladbroke Grove. I remember listening to him at pa and when he'd play it in the street at the Carnival. His voice was distir the talk-over because he mixed the melody of the song with the a talking and I enjoyed that. So I called him and he came to the studio morning – George gave him the words and he just toasted over Geo melody. We did a take and that was it, it worked."

Since then there have been a number of others, most notably Pickett, a keyboard player formerly with Sailor, who played keyboard the album and has now also worked with the band in writing se songs; Helen Terry, whose powerful, rich voice contributed to *Do Really Want To Hurt Me?* and more recently to *Church Of The Po Mind*; Terry Bailey (ex Teardrop Explodes) on trumpet; and Steve Grai (ex dole official) on sax.

But in the early stages, the band were still operating in atmosphere of great uncertainty and the pressure on Mikey's pers circumstances had not eased. "Things weren't going very well," explains. "All the money I had I was spending on the group and decided she just wanted to try something different. I explained to her, know, I couldn't go. I was dead against her leaving, because I could things were going to be happening with the band and life would be more comfortable in the next year. But she was adamant and she wen to America with the children. They live in New Mexico, in a place ca Santa Fe – it's a really nice place. Her mother bought a house out t and took everybody with her. The whole family has gone, just looking cooler vibes."

This also meant the end of Captain Crucial's involvement Culture Club. Mikey and Cleo have stayed in close contact and he visits children when he can; but, as is almost inevitable in such situations, M and Cleo have drifted apart. Mikey now has a new girlfriend, Tina. "S been good, because I need sorting out really. I need help to keep on rails, and she helps in that way." There seems little hope now of a reu with Cleo.

STEVE GRAINGER

PHIL PICKETT

HELEN TERRY

ond Culture Club photosession, 1981

21

トップ・スポット

top spot

SiNgLes by dave henderson

Culture Club 'Do You Really Want to Hurt Me' (Virgin) Third time lucky for George and the boys? Don't think so, this is weak watered down fourth division reggae. Awful.

Reviewed by Danny Baker

CULTURE CLUB: Do You Really Want To Hurt Me? (Virgin)
Culture Club astound me. They really are very very good indeed and yet, whilst slop like the pea-brained Haysi Fantayzee are rolling in it, this group reach their third fine record without a sniff of a hit. I recommended the last one 'I'm Afraid Of Me' which, I take it, must've stiffed while I was away in the land of rats and mongeese, Hawaii. 'Do You Really Want To Hurt Me' is similarly endorsed even though it takes the reggae form — light reggae though — and takes a couple of plays to make its shape fully known. Its B-side 'Love Is Gold' has a speed only previously attempted by Robert Palmer singing 'Looking For Clues'. (Fact confirmed by *Guiness Book Of Utah Salt Flat All Comer Rhythm Guitar Speed Attempts; Current Volume*). Both sides are fine, it's out on 12"; I don't see what else a poor group can do. Perhaps it's the spectre of the controversial sedan chair waving Boy George that keeps the public hemming and hawing. True, on the cover here he's pictured doing that clumsy embarrassing dance that our societies 'free-er' children alway feel prone to, that is, elbows out like a chicken and the old arse pushed out *in extremis* waving around in some positive statement to our undoubted African heritage. But they're a talented group; what can I tell you?

ALLAN JONES

CULTURE CLUB: "Do You Re[ally] Want To Hurt Me" (Virgin 7")
Boy George pouts prettily on th[e] sleeve and sings this fey ballad with all the camped-up theatric[al] gallumph of Kathy Kirby. Boy's performance here is hilariously

thespian, but lacks the sibillant lithp and bucketful of tears that would have made it unforgetta[ble].

The song itself is woefully ordinary, a familiar complaint, unremarkable whinge with a so[ft] underbelly. The shallow, anore[xic] white rasta riddums fail to ignit[e] any real spark of passion, settle instead for a glossy glide into th[e] fade.

Reviewed by ROBBI MILLAR

DEAD OR ALIVE 'The Stranger' (Black Eyes)
CULTURE CLUB 'Do You Really Want To Hurt Me' (Vrgin 7" and 12")

Pete Burns must be gnashin[g] his teeth over the recent successes of Culture Club and Haysi Fantayzee. After all, he was managing to look like a right Nancy long before any of these dread-locked imposters plus his single, an atmospheric grower with vocals that manag[e] to sound mournful rather than dismal, knocks spots off ditties about close encounters of the anal kind.

And it's aeons better than th[e] lily-livered Culture Club offering which starts off with overblow[n] Motown and quickly trips into the weakest sort of reggae. It's plain that the group's only ass[et] is the ludicrously unphotogenic (ignore the air-brushed sleeve) Boy George. God help 'em!

Reviewed by MARK COOPER

CULTURE CLUB: 'Do You Really Want To Hurt Me' (Virgin) How could anyone want to hurt the Boy George — we need him too badly. The reason for this is that he is a convincing victim of his emotions — George can still feel. This is a dreamy skank with rimshot drumming and a breathy vocal that proves that George refreshes the parts tha[t] other poseurs can't reach.

espite their lack of instant success, Virgin accepted the band's insistence that they had to keep putting singles out fast. So far, they sidered, they'd got through only to the hardcore; there were a lot more ple out there who'd never even heard of Culture Club.

"A lot of companies would have questioned us, slowed us down," Mikey, "but they didn't. They understood that we needed to get les out quickly to keep the interest, keep the flow. Something's always to be happening in the band – it's the nature of George's character."

They had already recorded the album, Kissing To Be Clever, ıding Do You Really Want To Hurt Me? which, like many of the songs, been developed from the basis of a melody and lyrics written by rge.

"George had this idea and he sang it to me," Jon explains. "He said vanted it reggaeish and I wanted it more lovers, a bit smoother than it turned out. Steve Levine, our producer, was there as well and he helped us out with a bit of the sound. So we had the words and the melody – not quite the same melody we ended up with. Then Roy put down the keyboards and that was really nice, though there were a few things that needed to be changed. Mikey got that brilliant bass line. And it's funny, when I went into the studio I didn't even know what I wanted to put on the track. So I just did it the way it came out – that was done in one take. And the rest was done in the studio where I did the mix with the producer."

Whatever the intricacies of writing and production were, it did the trick. Not only did it climb to the top in the UK – within a month or so they were clocking up the Number One slot in several different countries each week, and the gold discs started rolling in by the handful.

22 スウィート メロディーズ

sweet melodies

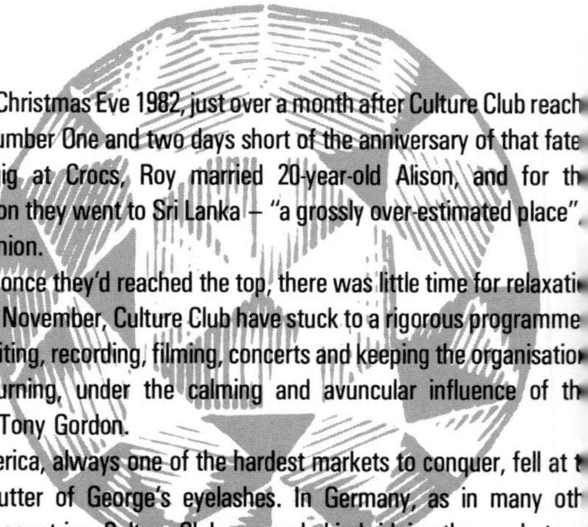

On Christmas Eve 1982, just over a month after Culture Club reach Number One and two days short of the anniversary of that fate second gig at Crocs, Roy married 20-year-old Alison, and for th honeymoon they went to Sri Lanka – "a grossly over-estimated place", Roy's opinion.

But once they'd reached the top, there was little time for relaxati since last November, Culture Club have stuck to a rigorous programme travel, writing, recording, filming, concerts and keeping the organisatio wheels turning, under the calming and avuncular influence of th manager Tony Gordon.

America, always one of the hardest markets to conquer, fell at t merest flutter of George's eyelashes. In Germany, as in many oth European countries, Culture Club succeeded in bridging the gap betwe the harshly divided rock and pop markets.

Among many other accolades, George became the Daily Mirro pop personality of the year.

Mirror
BOY

With brother Gerald

ボーイ・ジョージ

When *Do You Really Want To Hurt Me?* shot through the roof, four sets of parents stopped thinking that their sons were irretrievably lost to a no-hope dream. And if some retained their fears that pop is whimsical and insecure, they've no doubt been reassured by the worldwide success of the album, *Kissing To Be Clever*, and the following two singles, *Time (Clock Of The Heart)* and *Church Of The Poison Mind* – both of which, like *Do You Really Want To Hurt Me?*, were accompanied by entertaining and original videos.

"The *Time* video was good fun," says Mikey. "It was very childish. It's George's creation – it's good, it's warm. Again, it has that family feel. George needs to have that, he needs to be secure and he likes the family set-up. All four of us are sitting round drinking coffee and everybody's cup has got their name on it – Mikey, Boy, Jon and Roy, and the mum brings the cake in and puts it down and we're on the telly, and she goes – oooooh..."

Since their success, the band have had to be even more disciplined to continue making full use of their ideas. It's helped a great deal that their roles are so clearly defined and that each member of the band shares equally in profits and in important decisions. "It's very democratic," says Mikey. "We all make decisions for the band. One person might have the idea, but he comes to the rest of us and we work it out from there. No one person controls the band. We split everything right the way down the middle which is good, that reduces one pressure already."

George remains the most sought-after interviewee, but the others don't resent it. Says Roy: "We always knew it was going to be like that. George has charisma and that sets him apart. He likes to talk – and he's better at it than the rest of us. And he takes the pressure very well."

Mikey: "It doesn't really worry me that the press always want to talk to George and never to the rest of us. Business is straight, behind that crap. George is a good frontperson, that's his role in the band. I enjoy what I do and I recognise my position in the band – making music and playing it. In time I think they'll start wanting to do interviews with Roy or Jon or myself."

Jon: "You mustn't let your egos get in front of you. Sometimes I do, I get jealous of George. I think, fucking bastard, he's all over the papers, everybody loves him and nobody knows who I am... No, I'm only kidding. We all accept our roles. George is very good on the image and the artwork. The way he dresses, it's all natural to him. It's something I wish I had, but you've all got to know your own capabilities and with us it really works. If we were both like that it wouldn't work. Him and Malcolm (McLaren) were like that, millions of ideas all over the place, that's why they couldn't get on. But George has real talent. He could look normal, his dressing up is irrelevant. Of course, it's great and people love him, but above all it's his talent that shines through."

The discipline extends to the way they approach touring, which is a

'ith eldest brother Richard

Sporti 4
Subitar Lens
DACORA Kamerawerk

cry from Jon's days with The Damned. "None of us have drugs on the ad," says George. "And we don't drink alcohol while we're working. It's :ivilised situation and I really like it. I don't want to nurture the star thing.

"There's a very close relationship between all of us, it's almost like ving an affair. Mikey really annoys me, I have terrible rows with him. t I can't not, you know what I mean? I can't not call him a lazy slob, and calls me an ugly bastard, you know – you look really vile without your ake-up. There's ways and ways of being nasty, and I like the situation e're in."

Their roles remain as distinctive musically as they are ganisationally. "We each have different feels," Mikey points out, "so the usic will never be one set way as long as the four of us are working gether. Roy is mainly very balladish, Jon's quite rocky and I'm sort of reggaeish and funkyish. George sings sweet melodies normally and that's part of Culture Club now. We have to think of other melodies and chords to fit in with him, which is good. It's tricky, though."

After scores of live performances, they're still the same before each show – George and Roy extremely nervous, Mikey really cool and Jon – in Roy's words – "the old pro". George continues to produce more original ideas in a day than many artists do in an entire career. Culture Club still want to entertain everybody with warmth, and humour, and perhaps a touch of love.

And they still know where their strength lies.

Roy: "Our strongest point is that we can write good songs."

Mikey: "Good songs are our main concern. Just good, basic, simple songs . . ."

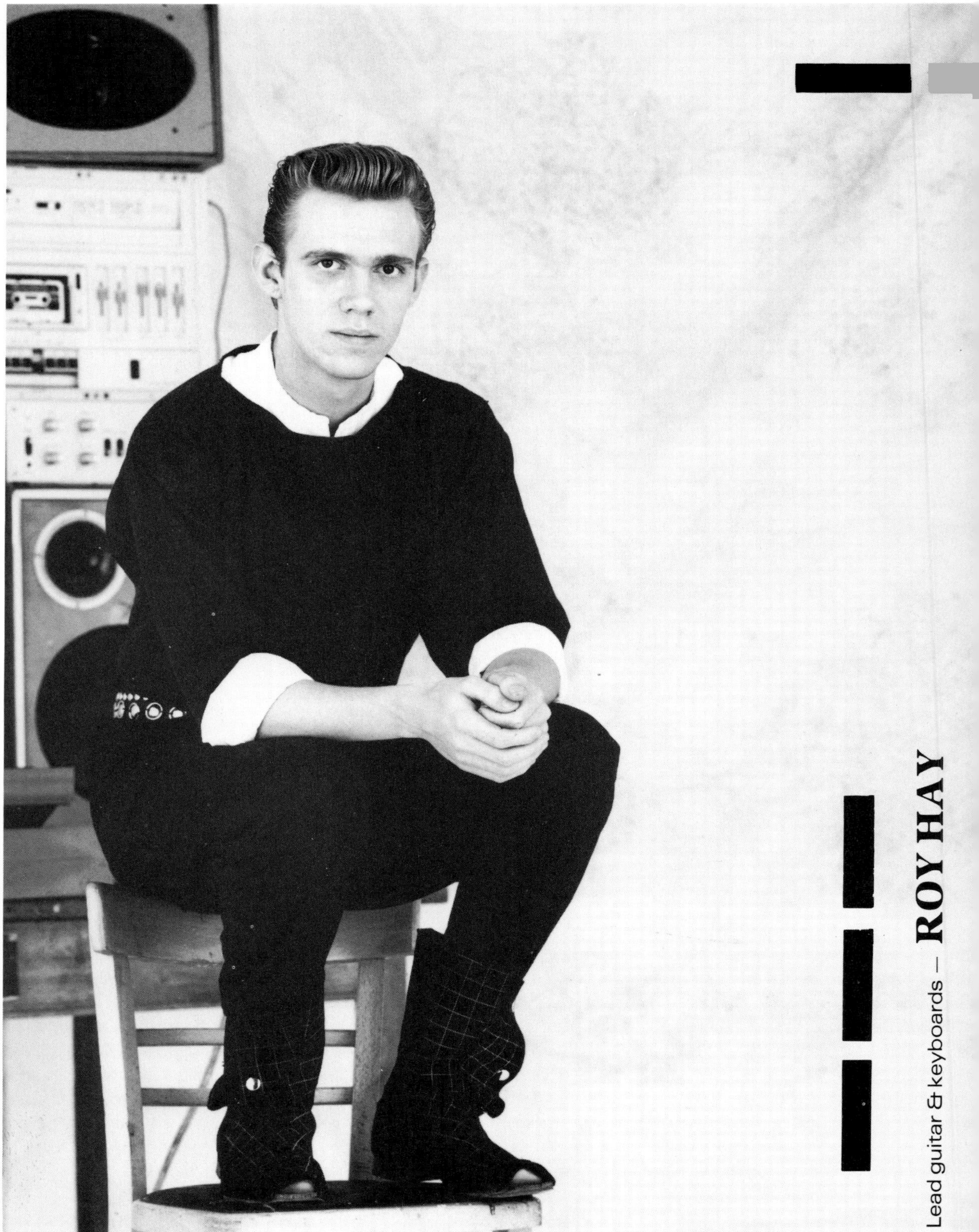

Lead guitar & keyboards — **ROY HAY**

Drums & percussion — **JON MOSS**

Bassguitar — **MIKEY CRAIG**

lanagement: **Tony Gordon**

AN CLUB
Culture Club
Wedge Music
63 Grosvenor Street
London W1

7-INCH SINGLES

21.5.1982	**A.** White Boy **B.** Love Twist	**VS**496
25.6.1982	**A.** I'm Afraid Of Me **B.** Murder Rap Trap	**VS**509
3.9.1982	**A.** Do You Really Want To Hurt Me? **B.** Do You Really Want To Hurt Me? (dub version)	**VS**518
19.11.1982	**A.** Time (Clock Of The Heart) **B.** White Boys Can't Control It	**VS**558
1.4.1983	**A.** Church Of The Poison Mind **B.** Man Shake	**VS**571

7-INCH PICTURE DISCS

3.9.1982	**A.** Do You Really Want To Hurt Me? **B.** Do You Really Want To Hurt Me? (dub version)	**VSY**518
19.11.1982	**A.** Time (Clock Of The Heart) **B.** White Boys Can't Control It	**VSY**558
1.4.1983	**A.** Church Of The Poison Mind **B.** Man Shake	**VS**571

12-INCH SINGLES

21.5.1982	**A.** White Boy **B.** Love Twist	**VS**496-12
25.6.1982	**A.** I'm Afraid Of Me **B.** Murder Rap Trap	**VS**509-12
3.9.1982	**A.** Do You Really Want To Hurt Me? **B.** Do You Really Want To Hurt Me? (dub version) + Love Is Cold (You Were Never So Good)	**VS**518-12
19.11.1982	**A.** Time (Clock Of The Heart) **B.** White Boys Can't Control It + Romance Beyond The Alphabet	**VS**558-12
1.4.1983	**A.** Church Of The Poison Mind **B.** Mystery Boy + Man Shake	**VS**571-12

ALBUMS

8.10.1982	**Kissing To Be Clever** **A.** White Boy (dance mix), You Know I'm Not Crazy, I'll Tumble 4 Ya, Take Control, Love Twist (featuring Captain Crucial) **B.** Boy, Boy (I'm The Boy), I'm Afraid Of Me (re-mix), White Boys Can't Control It, Do You Really Want To Hurt Me?	**V**2232
9.1983	**Colour By Numbers**	**TBA**

IS IT A HER? A HIM? - OR IS IT NEITHER?

Chart-busting singer has plunged rock world into confusion

The lead singer for the rock group 'Culture Club' is Boy George. The outrageous singer loves 'dressing up' and has inspired an army of youthful super-sissy imitators in Britain.

By MAURICE BENDER

England's top pop singer is a slinky songbird with powdered cheeks, ruby red lips and a sexy walk that drives the teen boys wild — and disgusts their parents.

British moms and dads are having fits because the bizarre lead singer of a chart-topping rock group IS A BOY.

Boy George, as he likes to be called, sickens adults by parading around like a floozie, his face painted with makeup and his shoulder-length black hair braided like Bo Derek.

"It wouldn't be so bad, but my 16-year-old son finds him attractive," said a London parent. "And America is next for this kind of punk rock sickness. It's spreading into other parts of Europe already.

"This kind of sexual mix-up could create an entire generation of homosexuals. Now where would that leave us!"

Others are convinced that the outlandish Boy George, whose hit record is "Do You Really Want to Hurt Me," is a menace to the country's youth.

"He's not just a bad example — he's disgusting. That thing's got all our children walking around wondering just which sex they are," said an upset mother.

Meanwhile Boy George, who likes to lounge around in a silk kimono with ribbons in his plaited hair, openly admits he enjoys "being a girl."

"Actually, I'm not really aware of my sexual identity," said the pop star.

"I sleep with both girls and boys but I'm neither proud nor ashamed of it.

"I don't think it's something to deny or be embarrassed over. People might think I'm weird — but I really don't have any sexual problem."

'Actually I'm not really aware of my sexual identity . . . I like people puzzling over whether I'm a boy or a girl'

Happy is what Boy George and the rock band Culture Club make thousands of teeny-boppers. They not only flock to his concerts and buy his records — but many are starting to dress and act like him.

Already, bustling English streets are dotted with teen boys sporting makeup, long, plaited hair and girlish wiggles. "Boy George is more than a singer — he's the future," gushed one male fan.

Tough judge is touched by little Kelli's cry for mercy

Child pens a letter of love

. . . and springs mom from jail

Little Kelli Edwards wrote a love letter that was so moving it melted the heart of a tough federal judge — and kept her mom out of jail.

"Please don't take her — she's the only mommy I have," Kelli, 11, pleaded. "Without her life just could never be any good at all for me and my two older brothers."

The little girl's mom, Lavesta Edwards, pleaded guilty to two charges of embezzling money from a credit union in Emmett, Idaho, where she worked.

She was awaiting sentencing when Kelli sent her touching letter to U.S. District Judge Hal Ryan.

"I, Kelli Edwards, age 11 — daughter of Lavesta Edwards — do want you to know I have the best mom there could ever be," little Kelli wrote.

"Without her, life can really get bad. Mom gives us her all every day. She never does anything for herself. We work darn hard around our place, but mom makes work something to do together. She makes it special.

"Without her, well, life just could never be good at all for us three kids."

Kelli lives with her brothers Kirk, 16, Shane, 14, her mom and her father, Gene. The family is very close, but in the past few years they've been scraping by.

In 1979, Lavesta embezzled $6,650 from the Boise Cascade Employees Credit Union. She was caught and convicted of the crime and could have received a lengthy prison sentence.

But because of little Kelli's loving letter — and 38 other letters from friends and relatives of the 38-year-old woman — Judge Ryan placed her on three years' probation.

The judge ordered the mother of three to pay back the money she embezzled and contribute 200 hours to a community service.

Then he sent her home to her determined little letter writer, Kelli.

— SUSAN JIMISON

Killed by sandwich bags

A 75-year-old woman died in a bizarre accident when an eight-ounce box of sandwich bags fell on her neck.

Doctors said the box — which was jostled off a grocery store shelf by a stockboy — critically injured Martha Dunham's spinal cord. She died two weeks later.

A jury ordered the store to pay the Pontiac, Mich., lady's family $187,000 for the tragic incident.

WEEKLY WORLD NEWS November 30, 1982 3

★★★★★★★★★★★★

Sun exclusive on pop's newest sensation

MISTER (or is it Miss?) WEIRDO

HE IS No. 1 in the charts and they call him the Gender Bender.

He is the sensational singer who looks like a girl, sounds like a fella and behaves like something strangely in between.

So when George O'Dowd fronts his group Culture Club on tonight's Top Of The Pops you can be forgiven if you are confused.

Is this prettily-painted creature with forty long lashes pouting over the microphone actually a bloke?

"I couldn't care less if people think I'm a girl," George, 21, says with a giggle.

I don't care if people think I'm a girl, says Boy George

By JUDY WADE

"I suppose I am actually bi-sexual. Or multi-sexual — because there's a lot to discover in life, y'know.

"But to clear up any doubts I call myself Boy George on my record."

Disc

And it is George's rich tuneful voice and not his freaky appearance that has carried his disc Do You Really Want to Hurt Me to the top of the charts.

"I get fans of both sexes," George says. "Actually I get more girls after me than the four straight guys in my band put together.

"I could pull them all if I wanted to, but at present I am not interested in sex at all.

"I'm working so hard at my career that I'm too exhausted by the time I fall into bed for any of that. I lost my virginity with a girl when I was 16 but sex has never been an obsession with me. It's just like eating a bag of crisps. Quite nice, but nothing marvellous. Sex is not simply black and white. There's a lot of grey.

"You can think what you like about me. I'm not bothered."

George's close-knit Irish Catholic family, now living in South-East London, are not bothered either.

He is third of five sons, has a younger sister, and the whole family is pleased and proud of his success. But younger brother Gerald, 18, an amateur boxer who works on a building site, admits that his mates often tease him about George's strange appearance.

He says: "They see him on Top Of The Pops and say, 'Your brother's bent. He's a poof, isn't he?'

"I just say, 'That's right. What of it?'"

Haircut

The brothers could not look more different. Gerald is well-muscled and clean-cut, with a squaddie's short-back-and-sides haircut.

George sits beside him in white Dracula make-up, slashed with blood-red lipstick.

Their mother, Dina, is 41 and, unlike her perfectly painted son, never wears make-up.

She says: "People do nudge each other and make awful comments when they see him. 'Doesn't he look like a girl?' they say to me.

"My answer is always, 'Yes. I'll bet a lot of girls would like to look as good as George does.'

"But I don't think he is homosexual. Anyway, who he chooses to sleep with is his business.

"He has always been such a loving son. He phones me every day and he visits us every weekend.

"When his dad had a heart attack he was so busy I didn't tell him until his dad was out of intensive care.

"He cried: 'You should not have done that mum.'"

George believes he may have inherited his love of dressing up from his dad, 48-year-old Gerald.

Sharp

He says: "When Dad was my age he was apparently a pretty sharp dresser.

"He had a huge quiff and liked pink shirts. But he used to moan at me about what I wore.

"Mum used to say to him: 'Do something, Dad — you can't let George leave the house like that.'

"And dad would roll his eyes to heaven and hide behind the newspaper.

"Now I think I am really close to both my mum and dad.

"They know that underneath all this make-up and the clothes I am pretty normal. Well, I think I am.

"For instance, my favourite telly show is Coronation Street and I love Hilda Ogden.

"My music isn't strange either — just ordinary romantic stuff. In fact, I'd be thrilled if Petula Clark decided to record one of them."

And you can't get any straighter than that.

Mrs DINA O'DOWD "He's such a loving son"

Boy George and boxer brother Gerald . . . still a closely-knit family PICTURE: STEVE LEWIS

23 ボーイ・トーク(3)

Boy talk (3)

"Love is a selfish thing. The minute you start thinki it's not you're very stupid, because you're satisfyi yourself in all ways — sexually and psychologically. Bu you can get the other person to enjoy you as well — gre

"I've had terrible relationships. Even now I ha violence, I have terrible punch-ups with people. I ne arguments, I need a sort of torrid relationship, I need swear and smash things and cry — not in a defeatist wa but in a positive way.

"I really slept around when I was younger, but n I've got a very strong moral code. More than anythin like being in love.

"Every relationship is as bad as the other, but it's way you deal with it that gets better. You never chan you've got basic ingredients in your character and th just remain for the rest of your life.

"I've never wanted to be sexual. I'm not sexy — attraction is my personality and I know that now. I nev knew that when I was younger, that I was a laugh. Whe was young I made girls laugh and that's what they like wasn't particularly beautiful; I had a cute face, but it w just that I was good to be with, I was fun. And I did realise it was because I was such a poof, you know. Gi relate to me in that way. They liked being with because they could talk about things. And also, it soun like an awful thing to say, but for a girl to have sex w someone like me isn't such a problem. You know wha mean? Because I'm not masculine, I don't want to be.

"There are other things apart from sex and physi contact and all those sort of things. You can be a lot mo attractive from your mind than you can be with yo body. I hate all that. I've never been on beaches, I h holiday resorts and shorts and running and muscles hate fitness. You can be fat, you can have a big nose, I you can be attractive in so many ways.

"I couldn't go to bed with someone just because th looked like a nice thing, you know, an object. We all ha that opportunity — now more so than ever. But none of wish to do it. We shouldn't take advantage of peop because it's not real, it's not yours, the way they're givi it to you is just a sick thing — why should they give it you because you're a pop star? I don't want it like tha

oy with Laura

BOY GEORGE CORRUPTS AMERICA SHOCK

"I don't think about whether people should be gay r straight, I really think that's pathetic. I hate the word isexuality. Sex is for everyone, everyone has their own ays of getting it. It's not wrong to fall in love with a man, 's just perfectly sane. There's worse things, there's ings that are just terrible. I mean, rape makes me feel ck, I just can't stand it. Because to me, your body is the ly real thing you possess, it's yours. And the thought of omeone taking that is like, I think I'd die, you know what nean? It's worse than shooting someone, because at least at's like, that's getting rid of you. Rape is like taking our soul away, it really is the most vile thing.

"I've got quite a big admiration for women, but I ink they're educated to make themselves weak. I hate e way women are used.

"So to me, although I've never thought about all is, now I like taking the piss out of my own sexuality, ecause it's like, haha, you know, is it a bird, is it a plane?"

***BOY GEORGE* turning US youth into homosexuals**

New Sounds New Styles, May 1982

Mikey with Kito and Amber

Mikey and Amos ('Captain Crucial') model Foundry wear.

THE FOUND

SSIONS

Culture Club

カメラがクレージー

24

カーテン

curtain

As the curtain falls on the London Dominion show, the fans gradually regain their composure. Within minutes, scores are at stage door awaiting a glimpse of the band. Others stream into enham Court Road and cause an instant traffic jam. The drivers blink scratch their heads, realising that a true description of this sight will ·r wash at home as an excuse for lateness.

For the band, Easter won't be much of a break. They must prepare · never-ending round of international trips while writing new material recording the second album. Within weeks they have another hit with ·rch of the Poison Mind. On midsummer night, with Time (Clock of the ·rt) at No. 2 in Billboard's US singles chart, Culture Club appear on ·nnel 4's Midsummer Night's Tube and announce that their ·ncoming album will be called Colour By Numbers. They plan a major to start late September.

The show goes on: in a frenzy. When Culture Club appear: cameras ·razy.

·nager Tony Gordon with George

スタンダード：インフォメーション

S:I

Kasper de Graaf and Malcolm Garrett are partners i the Standard:Information and Assorted iMaGe communication and design companies. They hav worked together since 1981, when Garrett becam design director of New Sounds New Styles, a month pop culture magazine edited by De Graaf. Thi magazine was the first to carry features and photo sessions on Culture Club and The Foundry. De Graa has worked as writer, editor and production editor o a number of publications in the music and arts fields Garrett handles the graphic design and packaging fo a wide variety of bands and has designed man books and art catalogues. De Graaf and Garret previously co-produced Duran Duran — Their story published by Proteus in December 1982.

Standard: Information *would like to thank the following —* ● Boy, Mum and Dad ● Mikey ● Jon ● Roy ● and their parents ● Tony Gordon ● Plaxy for spiritual sustenance ● Battling Bob Devereux for dextrous small print ● Cat for washing Malcolm's car ● Juliette Joseph for sending things to Paris ● Grace Zambini for a keen ear ● John Brown for entertainment and enterprise ● Dino ● Anne Crowley at Mitaka ● Cathy at QV ● Joe Ewart, Steven Appleby and Caryn Gough for Assorted iMaGes.

Library of Congress Catalog Card Number
ISBN 0=312=17879=4
First published in Great Britain by Virgin Books.
First US edition
10 9 8 7 6 5 4 3 2 1

● All photography and drawings supplied by Culture Club. Photographers include Mark Lebon, Didi Zill, Graham Smith, Perry Haines, Kate Garner, Pennie Smith, Bonnie Lippel, Ian McKell and Anton Corbijn.

● Drawings by Helen Connelly, Miyo, Liza Royce, Sunie & Alasdair, Rhonda, Natasha, Mandy, Nicola Garnall, Jacqui Conrie, Eleanor, Sharon Holloway, Selina Carr, D.N., Sue B. Caroline Blennerhassett, Frank, Charlotte Daniels, Char, Margo Borell, Frances Eastman, Natasa, Lynda Griffin, Nicole Dillbahner, Susan Esmont, Rachel, Minna, D.H.B., Margaret Dilks, Tanya Younes, Birgit Kutschenreuter, Rita Horrigan, Maggy, Tallulah, C. Schulze, Amanda Siegelson, Jeffrey Williams, John Storer, Fleur, Sarah George Kennedy Julia, M. Smith, Keri, Sally, Jane, Juliette, Tracy Fear, Toula, J.H., Greg, Julie Hardy, Tom Johnston, Kipper Williams, Helen Simpson, Judy Hatfield, Hiromi, Tracy Chivers, Jane Goldman & Sam, Diane. Special thanks to many others who sent drawings which could not be included due to lack of space.

● Produced and packaged by Standard: Information Ltd, 12C Curtain Road, London EC2A 3PJ. ● Typeset in Baskerville, Paladium, Rockwell, Univers and Zapf International by QV Typesetting, and The Printed Word. ● Japanese translation and typesetting by Mitaka. ● Production services by Book Production Consultants, Cambridge. ● Printed and bound in Great Britain by The Thetford Press, Thetford.